Launching the Writer's Workshop

3rd Edition

Grades 3-12

Kristina Smekens & Dr. Maureen Scane

Contributors | The Idea Team

Liz Shockey	Literacy Specialist, Smekens Education Solutions, Inc.
Linda Schmidt	Bright Elementary School (Bright, IN)
Nadine Gilkison	Digital Resource Designer, Smekens Education Solutions, Inc.
Kristi McCullough	Literacy Consultant, Smekens Education Solutions, Inc.
Courtney Gordon	Literacy Consultant, Smekens Education Solutions, Inc.
Sarah Ambler	Break-O-Day Elementary School (New Whiteland, IN)
Sherri Armstrong	Honey Creek Middle School (Terre Haute, IN)
Melanie Beaver	West Vigo Middle School (West Terre Haute, IN)
Amy Becker	Ridge Lawn Elementary School (Chicago Ridge, IL)
Stacy Callahan	St. Joseph-St. Elizabeth School (Ft. Wayne, IN)
Crystal Callaway	Bailly Elementary School (Duneland, IN)
Christie Campbell	Washington Township Middle School (Valparaiso, IN)
Deb Conley	Central Local School District (Sherwood, OH)
Kristina Connally	Highland Terrace Elementary School (New Haven, IN)
Christine Conner	Allen Elementary School (Marion, IN)
Cara Crickard	Bluffton-Harrison Elementary School (Bluffton, IN)
Karen Dexter	River Forest Junior/Senior High School (Hobart, IN)
Michelle Diehl	Churubusco Elementary School (Churubusco, IN)
Mary Feagley	Mount Vernon High School (Mount Vernon, IN)
Lori Hahn	Blair Pointe Upper Elementary School (Peru, IN)
Susan Hall	Brummitt Elementary School (Chesterton, IN)
Jenny Hanneman	Holy Family Catholic School (Jasper, IN)
Jessica Harper	Leo Elementary School (Leo, IN)
David Henry	Sweetser Elementary School (Sweetser, IN)
Michele Jablonski	Washington Township Middle School (Valparaiso, IN)
Claudia Jackson	Wilbur Wright Elementary School (New Castle, IN)
Susan Jernberg	Protsman Elementary School (Dyer, IN)
Jann Johnson	Indian Springs Middle School (Columbia City, IN)
Rebecca Johnson	Ralph Waldo Emerson School 58 (Indianapolis, IN)
Ruth Jostes	Lake Street Elementary (Crown Point, IN)
Barb Katenkamp	North Dearborn Elementary School (Guilford, IN)
Mary Kiningham	Cedarville Elementary School (Ft. Wayne, IN)
Barb Mahnesmith	Smoky Row Elementary School (Carmel, IN)
Kristin Mantta	Central Elementary School (Lake Station, IN)
Rebecca Meek	R.J. Baskett Middle School (Gas City, IN)
Jina Muncy	Sunman-Dearborn Intermediate School (West Harrison, IN)
Daniel Myers	Oaklandon Elementary School (Indianapolis, IN)
Jessica Meacham	Southern Door Elementary School (Brussels, WI)
Julie Meitzler	Bluffton-Harrison Elementary School (Bluffton, IN)
Tiana Perin	Eastbrook North Elementary School (Van Buren, IN)
Amy Pyle	Churubusco Elementary School (Churubusco, IN)
Nidzara Sakinovic	Heritage Elementary School (Monroeville, IN)
Staci Salzbrenner	Woodlan Elementary School (Woodburn, IN)
Kathleen Satterlee	Allen Elementary School (Marion, IN)
Alice Shorter	West Vigo Middle School (West Terre Haute, IN)
Sue Sipes	St. John-Emmanuel Lutheran School (Monroeville, IN)
Anna Spalding	Norwell High School (Ossian, IN)
Susan Speicher	Albany Elementary School (Albany, IN)
John Stoffel	Lincoln Elementary School (Huntington, IN)
Jane Strayer	Thomas Jefferson Middle School (Valparaiso, IN)
Melissa Taylor	Winfield Elementary School (Crown Point, IN)
Angie Thiery	Northside Elementary School (Hartford City, IN)
Trevor Thurman	Pendleton Elementary School-Intermediate (Pendleton, IN)
Veronica Tittle	Eastbrook North Elementary School (Van Buren, IN)
Rachel Williams	Davis Park Elementary School (Terre Haute, IN)
Jordana Zachara	Wallace Aylesworth Elementary School (Portage, IN)

We would not have been able to pull this project off if it weren't for the support of countless teachers and their students. We're grateful to our colleagues listed here who generously shared specific lesson ideas, classroom photographs, writing samples, and other resources.

Smekens Education Solutions, Inc. grants teachers permission to photocopy the reproducible documents included within the online resource. No other part of this publication may be reproduced in whole or in part, or stored in a retrieval system, or transmitted in any form without written permission from the publisher. For information regarding permission, write to Smekens Education Solutions, Inc., P.O. Box 332, Warren, IN 46792.

ISBN 978-0-9790186-8-8
Copyright © July 2008
by Smekens Education Solutions, Inc.

Second Edition © July 2010
Reprinted © September 2011
Third Edition © June 2017

Table of Contents

Overview | How to Use This Book

Although this resource is titled *Launching the Writer's Workshop,* it's really instructional lessons to teach writers all year long. The book is split into two parts— Part 1 is the "launch" to be executed during the first weeks of the school year, and then Part 2 provides lessons to teach writing the rest of the year.

PART 1: The First Weeks

The first seven sections (pp. 11-58) of this resource support a teacher in launching or starting a writer's workshop. They include numerous procedural lessons and writer strategies that are essential for establishing classroom management and building writer independence.

Depending on the grade level, this "launch" lasts three to six weeks.

Every grade level will *not* find all of the lessons within the first seven sections necessary or timely. Some of the lessons may be more appropriate later in the school year.

Some lessons are lower and slower and are a better fit for elementary writers. Others are a fast-paced review and therefore better for middle school or high school students. **The left columns on pp. 5-7 suggest beginning-of-the-year lessons most appropriate per grade range.** However, these are only suggestions. Skim them all and select those most relevant for the writers' needs.

There is a planning calendar on pp. 8-9 to build a schedule of "launch" mini-lessons and writing-time tasks from Sections 1-7. (A PDF and editable Word version of this planning calendar are available via the online resource.)

PART 2: The Rest of the Year

Sections 8-13 (pp. 59-125) include more than 50 detailed writing lessons and are organized by the 6 Traits of Writing.

However, these lessons should *not* be taught in the sequence they are presented in this book. Rather, spiral through them based on writer needs and the unit focus. Each section divider identifies the lessons with a P. I. E. distinction.

P **Lessons to PERSUADE** readers in opinion, persuasive, or argumentative writing.

I **Lessons to INFORM** readers in expository pieces, essays, compare-contrasts, research, etc.

E **Lessons to ENTERTAIN** readers in personal narratives and in written responses to reading.

Use the P. I. E. categories to help discern which lessons to target during different writing units.

Again, all the lessons in Part 2 are not applicable to every grade level. **The right columns of pp. 5-7 suggest *priority* lessons per unit.** This is a general pacing guide and skill progression. Again, it's just a suggestion; look at it as a starting point and customize as needed.

Remember, these priority skills are just a sampling of the lessons within all of Part 2. Some teachers may choose to add more mini-lessons or omit particular ones based on writer needs.

This icon, next to reduced images throughout the entire book, indicates the resources available @ *www.smekenseducation.com/Launch-3-12.html.*

There, teachers can download the full-sized lesson resources, writing samples, handout templates, Smartboard documents, PowerPoint presentations, Word templates, and more.

Launching the Writer's Workshop: Grades 3-12, Kristina Smekens and Maureen Scane
© 2017 Smekens Education Solutions, Inc.

Grades 3-5

PART 1: The First Weeks

Writing Topics

Setting Expectations

Creating Notebooks

Motivating Writers

Developing Spelling

Introducing the Traits

Building Rubrics

The list to the right represents the most essential writing skills teachers should address per writing unit. Take note that these are not *all* of the lessons within Part 2— just the most important ones for grades 3-5, according to the authors of this book.

The majority of these lessons fall within Section 8 (Teaching Ideas) and Section 9 (Teaching Organization). Each writing mode requires that the right information be arranged in the appropriate order. Therefore, skills from Sections 10-13 may be less of a priority when instructional time is limited.

PART 2: The Rest of the Year

Persuasive/Argumentative Mini-Units

Informative Mini-Units

Narrative Mini-Units

Grades 6-8

PART 1: The First Weeks

The list to the right represents the most essential writing skills teachers should address per writing unit. Take note that these are not *all* of the lessons within Part 2— just the most important ones for ELA grades 6-8, according to the authors of this book.

The majority of these lessons fall within Section 8 (Teaching Ideas) and Section 9 (Teaching Organization). Each writing mode requires that the right information be arranged in the appropriate order. Therefore, skills from Sections 10-13 may be less of a priority when instructional time is limited.

IMPORTANT: The suggested skills listed for grades 6-8 are based on foundational skills being taught in grades 3-5. If students lack that preparation, then middle school ELA teachers will likely need to teach mini-lessons noted in the lower grade-level scaffold on p. 5.

PART 2: The Rest of the Year

Launching the Writer's Workshop: Grades 3-12, Kristina Smekens and Maureen Scane
© 2017 Smekens Education Solutions, Inc.

Grades 9-12

The list to the right represents the most essential writing skills teachers should address per writing unit. Take note that these are not *all* of the lessons throughout Part 2— just the most important ones for ELA grades 9-12, according to the authors of this book.

The majority of these lessons fall within Section 8 (Teaching Ideas) and Section 9 (Teaching Organization). Each writing mode requires that the right information be arranged in the appropriate order. Therefore, skills from Sections 10-13 may be less of a priority when instructional time is limited.

IMPORTANT: The suggested skills listed for grades 9-12 are based on foundational skills being taught in grades 3-8. If students lack that preparation, then high school ELA teachers will likely need to teach lessons noted in the lower grade-level scaffolds on pp. 5-6.

Planning my Launch

School year:

Mini-Lesson:	Mini-Lesson:	Mini-Lesson:
Writing Time:	Writing Time:	Writing Time:
Mini-Lesson:	Mini-Lesson:	Mini-Lesson:
Writing Time:	Writing Time:	Writing Time:
Mini-Lesson:	Mini-Lesson:	Mini-Lesson:
Writing Time:	Writing Time:	Writing Time:
Mini-Lesson:	Mini-Lesson:	Mini-Lesson:
Writing Time:	Writing Time:	Writing Time:
Mini-Lesson:	Mini-Lesson:	Mini-Lesson:
Writing Time:	Writing Time:	Writing Time:

Launching the Writer's Workshop: Grades 3-12, Kristina Smekens and Maureen Scane
© 2017 Smekens Education Solutions, Inc.

PHASE 1: Identify writing topics	1-3 days	
PHASE 2: Establish writing procedures	5-10 days	
PHASE 3: Introduce the 6 Traits	6-12 days	
PHASE 4: Build a writing rubric	1-2 days	

		NOTES:
Mini-Lesson: Writing Time:	Mini-Lesson: Writing Time:	
Mini-Lesson: Writing Time:	Mini-Lesson: Writing Time:	
Mini-Lesson: Writing Time:	Mini-Lesson: Writing Time:	
Mini-Lesson: Writing Time:	Mini-Lesson: Writing Time:	
Mini-Lesson: Writing Time:	Mini-Lesson: Writing Time:	

Writing Topics

There are three common purposes for writing— to persuade (within persuasives/argumentatives), to inform (within informatives), and to entertain (within narratives).

Knowing that, support students in generating topics for those different writing purposes. Spend the first days of school filling up writers' notebooks with lists of potential writing topics that fit those different purposes.

Emphasize that writers need to stay within their individual topic territories. Many times, students select topics they are interested in but know little or nothing about. They choose to write about unfamiliar topics. Without additional research and study, the writing will inevitably be short and skimpy. They cannot develop what they don't know.

Lessons Appropriate Per Unit

Mini-lessons for
PERSUASIVE & ARGUMENTATIVE WRITING UNITS

P

#1	p. 12	Write for different purposes
#2	p. 13	Write about what you know
#4	p. 15	Generate ABC Chart topics
#5	p. 15	Springboard off other texts
#8	p. 18	Identify questions & concerns on a graffiti wall
#9	p. 19	List things wrong in the world

Mini-lessons for
INFORMATIVE WRITING UNITS

I

#1	p. 12	Write for different purposes
#2	p. 13	Write about what you know
#4	p. 15	Generate ABC Chart topics
#5	p. 15	Springboard off other texts
#8	p. 18	Identify questions & concerns on a graffiti wall

Mini-lessons for
NARRATIVE WRITING UNITS

E

#1	p. 12	Write for different purposes
#2	p. 13	Write about what you know
#3	p. 14	Create a memories picture collage
#5	p. 15	Springboard off other texts
#6	p. 16	Create a life line of experiences
#7	p. 17	Generate narratives in response to reading

Teacher Tip

The P.I.E. acronym is typically introduced within the reading curriculum. Students learn to infer the author's purpose for writing a particular text. However, P.I.E. is applicable during writing instruction, too. Students are the authors, and they are to write with intentional purposes.

Teacher Tip

The *P.I.E. Foldable* can serve as a place for students to take notes on the different characteristics of each mode throughout the year. Students can refer back to this resource, updating it with new information they learn.

Mentor Text

Further clarify the differences among the three modes by revealing three texts on the same topic—each with a different purpose.

P • Save the sea turtle brochure

I • Types of turtles

E • Ninja Turtles comic book

MINI-LESSON #1: Write for different purposes

Reveal several authentic and age-appropriate writings that are relevant to the students' everyday world:

- Birthday party invitation
- Magazine advertisement
- Restaurant place mat with kid games
- Classroom/school newsletter
- Sports article in local newspaper
- YouTube video tutorial
- Homework listed in agenda book
- School supply list
- Written explanation to a math answer
- Social-media photo/post
- Poster/Flyer hanging in the hallway
- Newspaper comics section
- College application essay
- College acceptance letter
- SAT study guide
- Anecdote revealed in a text message
- Song lyrics
- Movie or video game review
- Answer to end-of-chapter question
- Magazine article

Each of these was written for an intentional purpose. People write for a reason. Provide students with a copy of the *P.I.E. Foldable* and introduce the three major modes or purposes for writing.

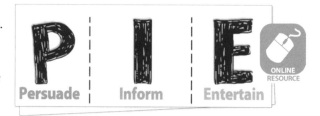

P = Write to persuade, influence, convince, motivate, argue, defend, critique, evaluate, or express a feeling or an opinion. Identify which of the real-world writing examples fall under this purpose (e.g., birthday party invitation, magazine advertisement, poster/flyer hanging in the hallway, movie or video game review, college application essay, etc.).

I = Write to inform, explain, teach, clarify, define, or demonstrate understanding. Identify which of the real-world writing examples fall under this purpose (e.g., classroom/school newsletter, sports article in local newspaper, YouTube video tutorial, homework listed in agenda book, school supply list, written explanation to a math answer, college acceptance letter, SAT study guide, answer to end-of-chapter question, etc.).

E = Write to entertain, convey a story, or share an experience. Identify which of the real-world writing examples fall under this purpose (e.g., restaurant place mat with kid games, social-media photo/post, newspaper comics section, anecdote revealed in a text message, song lyrics, magazine article, etc.).

Conclude this general overview explaining that students will experience all three modes of writing throughout the year.

Independent Writing:

Using the *Purposeful Writing Topics* handout, students brainstorm writing topics that fit each of the three purposes.

NOTE: Students are *not* writing any of the drafts today. Rather, they are simply listing topics they might write about on another day.

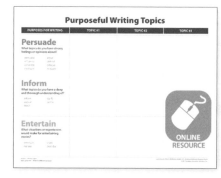

Launching the Writer's Workshop: Grades 3-12, Kristina Smekens and Maureen Scane
© 2017 Smekens Education Solutions, Inc.

MINI-LESSON #2: Write about what you know

Describe the light bulb that sometimes appears over a cartoon character's head and the fact that it represents he has an idea. Connect that concept to writing. When writers know about something, then they have an idea, and an imaginary light bulb appears over their heads, too.

Writers know about different things, and thus they have different "light bulbs" over their heads. When writers choose topics they have a lot of knowledge about, they can provide their readers with abundant information, numerous details, and specific insights that only someone "in the know" would include.

Model how to make a list of personal writing topics using the *I Know About* handout.

- *I am a parent. I could share lots of information about raising teenagers.*
- *I've done lots of fishing. I could share stories and even teach the reader about the best kinds of bait to use.*
- *I've had lots of experience at nursing homes. I could write about the important things I've learned about life from the elderly.*
- *I am a master at saving money at the grocery. I could tell story after story about how I got great deals.*

Inquire with students if they, too, have a deep knowledge of these same topics. (They probably don't— which is the point.) Reiterate that writers each have different "light bulb" topics. Although the teacher could write in great detail about these subjects, the students likely cannot… and should not. When someone attempts to write about a less familiar topic, the piece tends to be general in information and vague in details. Writers should always choose topics they know a lot about.

Independent Writing:

Provide students with the *I Know About* handout to make a list of topics they have personal knowledge on.

Visual Trigger

Purchase the Bright Ideas light bulb via the online resource.

Teacher Tip

Model topics that students cannot "steal" as their own. Make a list of topics and experiences unique to an adult and not ones that the average student would have had.

Teacher Tip

Rather than creating a paper list of writing topics, utilize the available technology and have students maintain a list of topics on Pinterest. With several pin-up boards on broad subjects, students could list smaller topics for future writings.

Follow-Up Lesson

It *is* possible to learn about an unfamiliar topic before writing about it. It's common that writers read and research topics they initially have little or no background knowledge on. This is the case when writing in the content areas and/or generating research reports.

MINI-LESSON #3: Create a memories picture collage

Spark students' personal memories using words and images. Each of these memories could be a future writing topic for another day.

Reveal a personal collage of topics. One by one, identify what the different images are within the collage and the personal stories they represent.

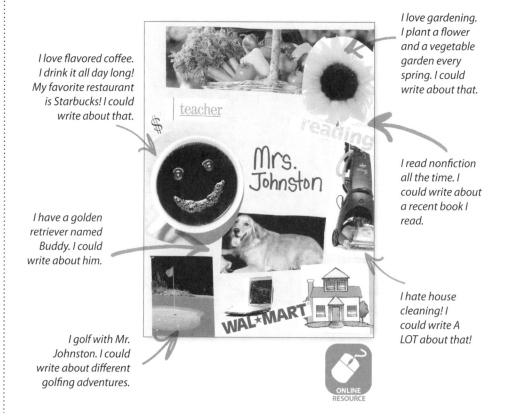

I love flavored coffee. I drink it all day long! My favorite restaurant is Starbucks! I could write about that.

I love gardening. I plant a flower and a vegetable garden every spring. I could write about that.

I read nonfiction all the time. I could write about a recent book I read.

I have a golden retriever named Buddy. I could write about him.

I hate house cleaning! I could write A LOT about that!

I golf with Mr. Johnston. I could write about different golfing adventures.

ONLINE RESOURCE

Independent Writing:

Identify the supplies (e.g., glue, scissors, markers, etc.) students will need and their source of images (e.g., magazines, catalogs, etc.).

Remind students that they are looking for images that represent topics they know about personally. These may include:

- Areas of expertise
- Known people
- Memorable events
- Favorite hobbies/interests
- Favorite games/activities
- Places been
- Unique talents or traits
- Lessons learned

Emphasize that everyone's memories and experiences are different, so the collages will all look different.

Launching the Writer's Workshop: Grades 3-12, Kristina Smekens and Maureen Scane
© 2017 Smekens Education Solutions, Inc.

MINI-LESSON #4: Generate ABC Chart topics

Model how to use the *ABC Chart* to log 26 writing topics.
- The teacher jots his/her name within the center of the chart.
- Note important people, places, and things within the letter boxes.
- More than one idea per letter is allowed, although the goal would be at least one topic per box.
- It's likely that the generated ideas may come out of order. Often one idea sparks another, although not alphabetically.

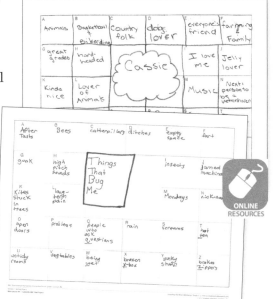

The first several topics come quickly, but when things slow down, Think Aloud about personal likes, dislikes, personality traits, characteristics, interests, memories, talents, etc. *What am I good at that others aren't? What do people say about me? What are things no one knows about me?* These answers provide potential writing topics.

Independent Writing:

Provide students with a paper or digital version of the *ABC Chart* to generate their own writing topics.

Teacher Tip

Model topics that students cannot "steal" as their own. Make a list of topics and experiences unique to an adult and not ones that the average student would have had.

Teacher Tip

This strategy can be repeated throughout the year using smaller, more focused subjects like "Personal Pet Peeves."

MINI-LESSON #5: Springboard off other texts

Start the mini-lesson with a list-book read aloud; see Mentor Text suggestions. Read the entire text quickly, showing the illustrations briefly.

Inquire if students had any text-to-self connections during the read aloud.
- *Did one page cause you to recall a particular personal event?*
- *Did one sentence remind you of a personal experience?*
- *Did any of the illustrations spark a memory in your mind?*

Invite students to share out briefly. Then explain that writers often find topic inspiration from other authors. A word, a sentence, a passage, even an illustration can remind a writer of a personal experience and identify a potential writing topic.

Independent Writing:

Students will listen to the text a second time. At the end of each page, pause for several moments. Students will make silent text-to-self connections based on the author's statement or illustrator's picture. They will consider a similar moment or circumstance in their own lives and jot it down in their notebooks as a potential writing topic.

Mentor Text

Favorite list books—
Cookies: Bite-Size Life Lessons,
   A. Krouse Rosenthal
The Important Book, M. Wise Brown
The OK Book, A. Krouse Rosenthal
One of Those Days,
   A. Krouse Rosenthal
Some Things Are Scary, F. Parry Heide

Follow-Up Lessons

Parody writers use one text as the inspiration for a second one. For more information, read "Teach Parody with Picture Books" via the online resource.

MINI-LESSON #6: Create a life line of experiences

The best narrative topics come from personal experiences. Reflecting on one's own life provides great fodder for story writing.

Model how to create a life line.

- Draw a horizontal timeline and label it *Life Line*.
- Recall several positive, enjoyable, happy memories. Explain that those "highs" are to be noted above the timeline (e.g., victories, vacations, holidays, milestones, etc.).
- Reflect on some negative, disappointing, sad memories. Explain that those "lows" are to be noted below the timeline (e.g., failures, bad-news moments, etc.).

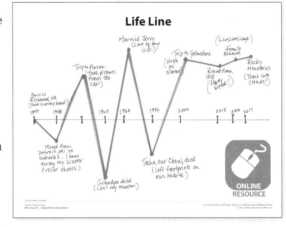

- Identify an early-in-life memory and whether it was a "high" or "low" event.
- Plot this first memory on the left of the timeline.
- Note the date and caption the significant moment. Provide only a gist statement— just enough to label the memory.
- Move down the timeline and mark the next notable memory.

Each of these "blips" on the life line represents an individual writing topic. Within the timelines, students will have numerous narrative stories that comprise their lives.

Independent Writing:

Provide students paper and colored pencils/markers to create their own life lines. End the writing time with students each marking three specific "blips" that would make for great narrative writings in the future.

NOTE: Using available technology, students could create a digital life line that includes inserting personal photos, videos, maps, etc. Consider the possibilities after watching the Google Chrome commercial within the online resource.

Follow-Up Lesson

Return to the life lines when beginning a memoir writing unit. Unlike a traditional personal narrative, a memoir doesn't focus on *what* happened as much as *how* it felt. A memoir is more insightful. It combines the feeling of a significant memory with the author's reflections. It digs below the surface details and incorporates the personal significance or impact.

Launching the Writer's Workshop: Grades 3-12, Kristina Smekens and Maureen Scane
© 2017 Smekens Education Solutions, Inc.

MINI-LESSON #7: Generate narratives in response to reading

Most standardized writing assessments are now rooted in reading. No longer are students writing personal narratives based on background knowledge. Instead, they are often asked to write a narrative in response to provided text(s).

Consequently, there will be many times when students are assigned a narrative writing task— and it's not one they have had personal experience with. This lesson provides an overview of five unique narratives that could be generated in response to a recent reading.

1. **Rewrite the story.** After reading a fictional text, students rewrite the same story, with the same basic plot, but told from a different character's point of view.

2. **Continue the story.** After reading a story, students write what happens next or predict how the characters will handle themselves the next time a similar situation occurs.

3. **Insert the missing.** There are places in texts where an author mentions an event but doesn't write out all the details. Perhaps an author references a phone conversation that was never detailed in the text. Or, the author may state that the character wrote a letter, but the actual letter is never revealed in the text. Within these products, students are to write only the missing portion or excerpt that would likely fit within the plot of the original text.

These first three narrative writing tasks are all based on literature. However, it's possible to write a narrative after reading informational text. The next two narrative tasks are fiction based on fact.

4. **Create historical fiction.** After reading an historical account, students write a story about a day in the life of someone living in that setting.

5. **Generate a sci-fi.** Students may read an informational text about a science concept and then have to incorporate the principles into the plot of a sci-fi story.

All five of these tasks require that students understand the plot structure of a story. Details about characters, settings, problems, and solutions are all pulled from the original text and incorporated into their narratives. The key is students are demonstrating they comprehended the original text. Unlike the traditional personal narrative that is based on the student's experiences, these stories rely solely on details from the assigned reading.

Independent Writing:

Identify recently read texts (literature or informational). As a class, and using the details from the original texts, brainstorm possible story plots that would fit the various narrative types. Remind students that a plot must have a problem/conflict and a solution/resolution.

Video Clip

For more information about this lesson concept, watch "Generate Narratives in Response to Reading" via the online resource.

Teacher Tip

Connect the reading and the writing curricula. Tie narrative writing tasks directly to the content learned from literature and informational text.

MINI-LESSON #8: Identify questions & concerns on a graffiti wall

Discuss what students know about a wall of graffiti. Comments might include:

- *There is a purpose or message within the graffiti.*
- *The message is visual and often colorful.*
- *The writing is skewed and haphazard, adding to the "art" effect.*

With a common understanding of the term "graffiti wall," now introduce the notion of building an all-class version. Announce that students will generate a visual collection of things they wonder about— confusions they have, problems that exist, questions they want answers to, etc. Explain that this wall of headlines and visuals will serve as topic inspiration for their next research paper, persuasive writing, or argumentative essay.

Model how to identify a graffiti-wall item using magazines and newspapers.

- Study the headlines, photos, articles, advertisements, etc.
- Think Aloud about possible controversial, political, environmental, and social issues. Go beyond the literal meanings of the images and ideas and consider different perspectives, possible problems, potential outcomes, etc. (This is like the book springboard concept explained in Mini-Lesson #5, p. 15.)

- If the word/image causes some questions, cut it out and adhere it to the graffiti wall. (This is like the memory picture collage explained in Mini-Lesson #3, p. 14.)
- Consider adding a short caption or question to label the image or word.
- Repeat this process, identifying additional items for the graffiti wall.

ONLINE RESOURCES

Together, students will build an eclectic mix of high-interest topics. In the near future, each student will identify one of the issues from the graffiti wall to be the subject matter of an informative, persuasive, or argumentative writing.

Independent Writing:

Identify the wall space or bulletin board (covered with poster board or butcher paper) that will become an all-class graffiti wall. Provide an assortment of magazines and newspapers for students to sift through. Also set out any needed supplies (e.g., glue, tape, scissors, markers, etc.).

Teacher Tip

Post the graffiti wall for several days/weeks. This will be the source of inspiration for future research topics. During this time, some students might abandon their original topics and need to use the wall to identify new ones.

Teacher Tip

Each class period adds to the same graffiti wall of topics. Have plenty of magazines and newspapers in reserve. After the first several classes/periods, the original resources will be pretty well picked over.

MINI-LESSON #9: List things wrong in the world

In anticipation of an opinion, persuasive, or argumentative writing unit, students need a clear understanding of what counts as a debatable topic.

Informative writing explains a topic or issue. But persuasive/argumentative advocates for a position on a topic or issue. More than just telling the reader information, this writing influences, convinces, persuades, or motivates the reader. The writer is defending, arguing, or claiming that one perspective is better than another. This means the argued topic has to have multiple sides; it must be debatable.

To do this, begin identifying topics that students have strong opinions about. Reveal the *Things Wrong in the World* handout. Brainstorm topics that come to mind for the various categories:

- Rules to change
- Things you want/wish for
- Problems to fix
- Things to change
- Injustices all around
- Favors to ask
- Suggestions to make
- Things not fair
- People to help

Things Wrong in the World

RULES TO CHANGE: FAVORS TO ASK:

THINGS TO WANT/WISH FOR: SUGGESTIONS TO MAKE:

PROBLEMS TO FIX: THINGS NOT FAIR:

THINGS TO CHANGE: PEOPLE TO HELP:

INJUSTICES ALL AROUND:

Independent Writing:

Use a portion of the writing time for students to identify topics per category. Then, when idea-generation slows, lead the class on a silent field trip. Walk them throughout the school building, encouraging them to observe their world as writers. *Whom do they see that you could help? What do you see that needs fixing? What situations seem unfair?*

Take them to familiar places within the building (e.g., the gymnasium, main office, cafeteria) and to some less familiar ones (e.g., the boiler room, the teachers' lounge, behind the kitchen counter). What do they see, question, or wonder?

While participating in this silent field trip, students are looking for situations that they have opinions about. They make note of them within their *Things Wrong in the World* handouts.

Mentor Text

Introduce students to the concept of debatable topics via read alouds.

LITERATURE
Some picture books develop multiple character viewpoints within the same story line.

Click, Clack, Moo, Cows That Type, D. Cronin
The Day the Crayons Quit, D. Daywalt
Duck! Rabbit! A. Krouse Rosenthal
Hey, Little Ant, P. Hoose
Voices in the Park, A. Browne

INFORMATIONAL TEXT
Each of these texts presents two viewpoints on the same topic or event.

Perspectives Flip Books series—
  Animal Testing
  Punishing Bullies
  School Lunches
  Social Media

The Split History series—
  American Revolution, M. Burgan
  Battle of Gettysburg, S. Fitzgerald
  Civil Rights Movement, N. Higgins
  Civil War, S. Fitzgerald
  Westward Expansion, N. Musolf
  Women's Suffrage, M. Burgan
  World War I, M. Burgan
  World War II, S. Rose

Teacher Tip

For added inspiration, students can look throughout *www. procon.org*. This website is a hub of debatable topics.

Setting Expectations

Well-run writer's workshops do not just happen. They are the by-product of procedural lessons and expectations set early in the school year. Such lessons will consume precious instructional time at the beginning of the year, but they're worth it.

Keep in mind that these students had a different teacher last year who had a different set of routines and procedures. Without new writer expectations outlined for *this* year, students may pull on the habits learned previously— and they may not all be good ones.

Procedural Mini-Lessons

Video Clip

For information about managing a writer's workshop within a MS/HS classroom, watch "Juggle Reader & Writer Workshops in 50 Minutes" via the online resource.

Video Clip

After a writing skill is taught in a mini-lesson, it can be practiced as bell work. Watch "Explore Bell-Ringer Options" via the online resource.

Teacher Tip

After each procedural mini-lesson within Section 2 (pp. 21-26), students are to select a writing topic from their brainstormed lists (Section 1, pp. 11-19) and write independently.

MINI-LESSON #1: Meet for daily instruction

Announce to students *It's time for writer's workshop.* The first part of the workshop is an all-class meeting called the mini-lesson.

Describe the teacher's role during the daily mini-lesson.
- To teach students something about writing/writers.
- To reveal the skill done well in anchor papers and/or mentor text.
- To give students an opportunity to talk through examples of the skill before having to execute it themselves.
- To tie the skill to a concrete object or trigger.
- To relate the skill to one of the 6 Traits of Writing.
- To keep it short and "mini" so students have time to write afterwards.
- To present the lesson in an engaging way (e.g., fun delivery, funny writing samples, visual triggers, etc.).

Describe the students' role during the mini-lesson.
- To listen to the instruction.
- To participate when the lesson becomes interactive.
- To think about how the lesson applies to their own writings.

Outline the logistics of the mini-lesson.
- Identify where the lesson will occur.
- Explain that the lesson will last 15 minutes or less.
- Describe any materials (e.g., notebook, pencil, laptop, etc.) that students should have ready.

Maximize the efficiency and efficacy of the mini-lesson with code phrases.
- Introduce *Turn and Talk* as the portion of the mini-lesson when students will turn to a nearby student and experiment with the skill in oral writing.
- *Back to Me* signals when students should quickly conclude their talk time and prepare to share out their attempts with the class.

Independent Writing:

Students select a writing topic from their brainstormed lists (Section 1, pp. 11-19) and write independently.

Launching the Writer's Workshop: Grades 3-12, Kristina Smekens and Maureen Scane
© 2017 Smekens Education Solutions, Inc.

MINI-LESSON #2: Describe the writing time

Brainstorm the meaning of a workshop. Identify it as a place where things are created, built, and/or fixed. Explain that after every mini-lesson, there will be a workshop time. This is when the students will create, apply, or practice something in their writing.

This second part of the writer's workshop begins when the teacher announces the code phrase— *Now it's your turn.* This signals to students that it's time to move from teacher instruction to independent student writing time.

Describe the atmosphere expected during independent writing time.

- Students work at their desks/tables executing the task identified at the end of the mini-lesson.
- Students work independently, unless the task requires a partner or group effort.
- Students may get up to retrieve supplies, share with a peer, etc.
- The teacher moves throughout the room conferring, helping, complimenting, etc.
- If a student needs support when the teacher is unavailable, he utilizes the Help! Tent/Strip (Mini-Lesson #5, p. 25).

One big facet of the writing time is knowing how long it will last. It's typical that this "workshop" time is shorter at the beginning of the year but gets longer as writer stamina grows. Identify a way to indicate how long writing time will last each day.

Independent Writing:

Students select a writing topic from their brainstormed lists (Section 1, pp. 11-19) and write independently.

Teacher Tip

Some teachers prefer that students dive into writing time without the option of talking with a peer immediately. This might be referred to as "silent writing time." Then, after several minutes of uninterrupted writing time, announce that it's "quiet writing time," giving students permission to seek out peers, if and when they are ready for feedback.

Teacher Tip

When students are writing, the teacher might also write to model the behavior expected.

MINI-LESSON #3: Outline sharing time/Author's Chair

Explain that at the end of writing time each day, there is another meeting. This one is devoted to celebrating the writing students created that day.

To move into the third portion of the writer's workshop, introduce another code phrase— *Wrap it up*. This indicates that writers should put away their notebooks and prepare for Author's Chair.

Outline the procedures.

- Explain that 1-3 sharers are selected based on accomplishments during that day's writing time. The teacher will indicate the portion of the writing the student will read aloud.
- Identify the actual chair (e.g., stool, teacher's chair, rocking chair, etc.) or explain if "Author's Chair" is a figure of speech that simply means the student has the floor.
- Explain that the teacher will introduce each sharer, identifying the student, the piece, and the skill the class should listen for. Then that student will read aloud only the portion requested.
- With only 1-3 students sharing a portion of their writing, Author's Chair will last approximately five minutes each day.

Independent Writing:

Students select a writing topic from their brainstormed lists (Section 1, pp. 11-19) and write independently. NOTE: Students might choose to continue working on a previously started piece.

While observing students as they write, select 1-3 writers to read during Author's Chair. Consider students who have chosen topics that they obviously know a lot about. This reinforces a recently taught writing skill (Mini-Lesson #2, p. 13).

Teacher Tip

Sharing time is not "show and tell." Asking for volunteers often garners kids reading lengthy pieces that are not necessarily strong. Assigning students to share on particular weekdays (regardless of what they wrote) isn't purposeful. Rather, use the Author's Chair as an opportunity to point out specific skills and successes.

MINI-LESSON #4: Review the 3 Parts of a writer's workshop

Review the three parts of the writer's workshop, including expectations, procedures, and code phrases:
- *It's time for writer's workshop* (Mini-Lesson #1, p. 22).
- *Now it's your turn* (Mini-Lesson #2, p. 23).
- *Wrap it up* (Mini-Lesson #3, p. 24).

Independent Writing:

Students select a writing topic from their brainstormed lists (Section 1, pp. 11-19) and write independently.

Teacher Tip

If students have participated in a writer's workshop for several years, consider executing this mini-lesson in lieu of three separate ones.

Launching the Writer's Workshop: Grades 3-12, Kristina Smekens and Maureen Scane
© 2017 Smekens Education Solutions, Inc.

MINI-LESSON #5: Support writers when they need help

It is inevitable that students will need help during the writer's workshop when the teacher is unavailable. Anticipate and troubleshoot this situation.

Provide each student a Help! Tent or Help! Strip. Explain that when in need of help, they simply display it on their desks.

However, the Help! Tent/Strip alone isn't very effective. The key to this lesson is the list of strategies to keep students writing even when they're stuck.

For the Help! Tent, review the strategies listed on the backside. *While I am waiting, I will...* implies that students are NOT doing nothing! Discuss each task listed. Review the previously learned skills/strategies that students could apply while waiting. Explain that if students accomplish one task and the teacher is still busy, they should choose another one.

For the Help! Strip, the procedure is the same. However, students will help generate the list of tasks *and* note them on their personal Help! Strips. Common strategies might include:
- Quietly ask another student for help.
- Skip a couple of lines and keep writing.
- Reread and add three details.
- Replace 3 weak words for WOW! words.
- Work on a previous writing.
- Start a new piece.

Point out that none of the options on the tent/strip suggests students "sit and do nothing."

Independent Writing:

Students continue working on the piece they started previously or start a new free-choice piece. During writing time, seek out those who use the Help! Tent/Strip to indicate that they need support.

At the conclusion of writing time, praise students who are utilizing the tool appropriately; troubleshoot as necessary. Let all students know where to store their Help! Tents/Strips.

HELP!
I have a question, but I can keep on writing.

Help! Tent

While I am waiting, I will...
1. Ask another student for help.
2. Skip a few lines and keep writing.
3. Reread and add three details.
4. Change four weak words to WOW! words.
5. Work on a previous writing.

ONLINE RESOURCES

HELP!
I have a question, but I can keep writing.

1. Ask another kid
2. Skip some lines + keep going
3. Add 3 more details
4. Circle 4 teeny words + replace
5. Check sentence beginnings, repeats?
6. Check out what others are doing
7. Edit my stuff
8. Go back to a previous writing.
9. Start something new.

Help! Strip

MINI-LESSON #6: Hold teacher-writer meetings

Discuss various meetings students may have attended (e.g., sports/team meetings, student/class council meetings, club meetings, etc.). Identify the general outline of such meetings— several people attend, specific item(s) are discussed, a plan is determined, tasks are assigned, and the meeting ends.

Explain that during writing time, the teacher will host several meetings with groups of students. These conversations will all be about their writing.

Outline the logistics of a conference.
- The teacher will meet with a *group* of students, not individuals.
- A "group" is a cluster of 3-5 students sitting near one another.
- No one will read his entire piece during the group conference. Rather, the teacher will indicate what portion students will read aloud.
- Each group meeting will last approximately five minutes.
- The goal would be to meet with every group during every writing time. However, if time runs out, the teacher will begin with the next group the following day.

Reveal the rhythm of a group conference:

1. Invite students to each read a portion of their current writing. (See the *Conference Starters* for suggestions.)
2. After all students within the group have shared, offer each student a specific *Conference Compliment*. If the same compliment applies for multiple students, say it once. This is also when an invitation to Author's Chair may be offered (Mini-Lesson #3, p. 24).
3. Provide a specific comment per student. Consider the one change/addition that would make the biggest impact on the writing. If the same suggestion applies for multiple students, say it once.
4. Conclude the group conversation with *What will you do next?* This encourages them to continue writing as the conference ends.

Model appropriate writer-conference behaviors and offer pointers to make the meetings efficient.
- *Don't act surprised to see me. You know I'm coming!*
- *Look at my eyes when you're talking to me and/or listening to me.*
- *Speak clearly; don't mumble.*
- *If I asked you to show me something in your writing, point to it.*
- *When I ask a question, never answer "I don't know."*

Independent Writing:

Students start a new writing or work on a previous day's piece. During the writing time, apply the 4-step rhythm to group conferences. (Remember to invite 1-3 students to share for Author's Chair.)

Teacher Tip

Writers would rather have a couple of minutes of teacher feedback every day versus 20 minutes once a month.

Teacher Tip

Writers can absorb 1-2 comments per conversation. That said, telling a student numerous things to change or fix within his draft is futile. He didn't absorb or understand all that was said, let alone remember each suggestion.

Teacher Tip

In between group conferences, look for Help! Tents/Strips (Mini-Lesson #5, p. 25). Answer those individual questions and then move on to the next group conference.

Creating Notebooks

A writer's notebook is more than a journal or diary. It's more than a folder to store loose papers and editing checklists. A writer's notebook is a personal space for writers that serves three main functions: collecting, generating, and organizing.

Writers collect lists of favorite words and potential topics within a writer's notebook. It's also a place to generate writing. Whether writing a complete product or just experimenting with language, the notebook is where these pieces are stored.

Finally, the notebook is an organizational tool. The writer maintains resources, lists, and other reference tools for quick access.

Instructional Insights

pp. 28-29	Consider format options for writers' notebooks

Procedural Mini-Lesson

#1	p. 30	Introduce the writer's notebook

Consider format options for writers' notebooks

1. **A three-ringed binder** allows pages to be inserted and moved throughout the sections. It's very flexible. However, dividers can be expensive, and the binder itself consumes a lot of space in a student's desk or on classroom shelving. Plan for storage options.

2. **A spiral notebook or a marbled composition book** is great for eliminating the flurry of loose papers. However, as is, this format doesn't allow for much flexibility in revision, short of ripping out the pages.

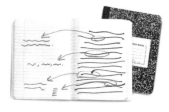

To make these bound books a little more functional, add pockets and a bookmark. Also, utilize right and left-hand pages purposefully (Mini-Lesson #2, p. 33).

3. **A digital notebook** is becoming more popular. There is a variety of software and storage possibilities, not to mention the online research capabilities. However, consider carefully if starting the year with a digital notebook is best. With technology comes another layer to instruction.

Students will need instruction on how to download apps, upload documents, where to save, how to save, and what to save, etc. Often the intended emphasis on writing is secondary to the technology lesson when digital notebooks are introduced too early.

If students' tech knowledge is minimal, consider waiting to introduce a digital notebook until after procedures are in place and the workshop is up and running.

Launching the Writer's Workshop: Grades 3-12, Kristina Smekens and Maureen Scane
© 2017 Smekens Education Solutions, Inc.

Consider format options for writers' notebooks, *continued*

4. Multiple pocket folders "bound" together offer section organization without the space needed to store a large binder.

Purchase 3-4 paper pocket folders. Cut one along the spine to create the front and back covers. Keep all remaining pocket folders whole; do not cut them. Fold each of these inside-out, putting the center crease on the *outside*.

Purchase one pocket folder with tabs and additional pocket folders without tabs. Turn the tab-less folders inside-out and hole-punch them. Using the tabs, fasten the folders together.

Suggested writer's notebook sections include:

- **Topics & Ideas Section**— Idea and topic lists generated during the first days go in this section/pocket.

- **My Writing Section**— Partial drafts, dabblings, and experiences go in this section/pocket.

- **Works Under Construction/Revision Section**— Store longer "assignments" or pieces that will go through the writing process.

- **Abandoned Writings Section**— Occasionally clean out the *My Writing* section. Instead of throwing away half-drafts and dabblings, students put them into this "abandoned" section. These pieces are used to practice grammar within the context of the student's own writing.

- **Wow! Words Section**— Writers collect words (e.g., sensory word lists, synonym lists for *said*, transition word lists, action verb lists, etc.). Store these in this section for quick retrieval and reference.

- **Writing-About-Reading Section**— Notes collected from reading and the after-reading written responses go here.

- **Content-Area Writing Section**— Writing done in math, science, and social studies should be held to the same high expectations as that done within the writer's workshop/language arts class. Send that message by maintaining all writings in the same resource.

- **Helpful Hints Section**— Editing checklists, writing rubrics, grammar rules, proofreading marks, mini-lesson notes, etc. will be stored in this section/pocket of the writer's notebook.

Teacher Tip

Access photo-based directions for how to compile these writer's notebooks via the online resource.

Teacher Tip

Determine the different items students will house within their notebooks. For example, if reading responses and content-area writings are also stored within the writer's notebook, then there needs to be additional sections. (Every pocket folder purchased adds two more sections to the notebook.)

Teacher Tip

Regardless of the format or structure, these are common sections within any writer's notebook. They can be found within 3-ring binder notebooks, composition notebooks, and digital notebooks, too.

MINI-LESSON #1: Introduce the writer's notebook

Unveil the writers' notebooks; make them a big deal. Consider how to present them in a special way. The more valuable the teacher makes the writers' notebooks, the more the students will cherish them.

Convey the importance of this notebook and its integral part within the writer's workshop. It's not just a storage mechanism; it's where students will experiment and ultimately learn to write.

After each student has his notebook, the teacher might open one and describe what it will look like by the end of the school year. Describe what might be on different pages and/or in different sections/pockets. *By the end of the year, this will be full of writing-topic ideas and favorite sentences collected from mentor text. It'll have lots of first-starts and writing experiments but many longer pieces, too. There will be stories, letters, reports, and even poems. This is where you'll learn new punctuation, capitalization, and grammar skills. It's not just a place to write but also to keep all the documents important to writers (e.g., Help! Strips, rubrics, etc.). And all of it is together in one place— within your very own writer's notebook.*

Identify the different sections/pockets and have students create/label them. Pass back any topic lists or writings generated from the previous days. Students will sort and organize them into their proper sections.

Address additional logistics:
- Identify where notebooks are stored (e.g., within their desks, on a book shelf, within a crate, etc.).
- Describe when students should retrieve their notebooks (e.g., before or after the mini-lesson, at the beginning of class, etc.).

Independent Writing:

Reiterate that notebooks contain the thoughts and writings of individuals. Thus it makes sense that not only the content is personal, but the exterior should also reflect the writer's individual self.

Give students the opportunity to personalize their writers' notebooks. Provide the supplies to decorate the covers. Not only will this increase their individual ownership, but students will more easily recognize their notebooks among all the others when stored in the classroom.

Teacher Tip

As students bring in their writer's notebook supplies at the beginning of the year, collect them. Then, when it's time to present this lesson to the class, the teacher can unveil them and increase the excitement level.

Teacher Tip

Students' notebooks are the core of the writer's workshop; they need them every day. Consequently, it may be necessary to store them within the classroom.

Teacher Tip

Additional tips include:
- Students generate a table of contents and number each page for spiral-bound/marble composition notebooks.
- Students label the sections of the pocket folders with stickers.
- Students may set up their digital notebooks, saving them to the server or the cloud.

Teacher Tip

If the writer's notebook is a spiral-bound or composition notebook, the writing time may be spent taping on ribbon bookmarks or gluing together page-pockets (p. 28).

Teacher Tip

The decorated cover could be a memory picture collage (Mini-Lesson #3, p. 14) and serve as a visual list of future writing topics.

Launching the Writer's Workshop: Grades 3-12, Kristina Smekens and Maureen Scane
© 2017 Smekens Education Solutions, Inc.

Motivating Writers

Lucy Calkins says it best: "When you're done, you've just begun." However, for many students, writing is not a process— it's a chore. They want to do just enough to be "done." The lessons within this section refute that thinking with strategies that build essential writer habits.

Simply telling reluctant or unmotivated writers to reread and make their drafts better is too vague. Motivate "done" writers with supplies and tools. Improve peer-conference conversations with focused questions. Provide explicit actions for students to take in self-revision and self-editing.

Teach specific next steps so students know what to do when they *think* they are done.

Revision Mini-Lessons

Editing Mini-Lessons

Instructional Insights

MINI-LESSON #1: Establish a "Done" list

When students complete a draft, they need some direction in order to self-revise. Explain that it's common to come to a stopping point but not to confuse that with being done.

However, a generic *Reread and make it better* declaration doesn't provide enough motivation. "Done" writers are task-based students; they are git-r-done writers. Knowing this, build an explicit list of revision tasks that cause students to re-enter their writing. This is referred to as the "Done" list.

Start a "Done" list including explicit tasks that students already know how to do; they just need to be reminded. For example:

1. *Start a new piece.*
2. *Work on a previous piece of writing.*
3. *Read your writing to a classmate.*
4. *Insert three details (words or phrases) with a blue pen.*
5. *Strikethrough four "dinky" words with a purple pen and replace them with WOW! words.*

Identify specific tasks that require writer tools (e.g., colored pens, sticky notes, highlighters, etc.). The "fun factor" increases when students get to revise with writer tools and supplies. See Mini-Lesson #2, p. 33 for more information.

If there are certain tasks that every student *must* do, then label those with the *must*ard icon. However, the majority of the self-revision tasks are choice-driven—things they *may* (*mayo*) want to do.

Acknowledge that *Sit and do nothing* is not an option on the "Done" list. During writing time, students must re-enter their drafts or work on another piece.

Post the initial "Done" list on a classroom wall chart. (It needs to be a physical resource accessible in the environment.)

Independent Writing:

As students "finish" their drafts, they are to apply a variety of revision tasks from the "Done" list. During Author's Chair, have two or three students share what they did after they initially thought they were "done."

Teacher Tip

Encourage revision strategies, rather than editing strategies, within the "Done" list. Keep this list focused on the sound of the message. Therefore, the strategies listed should target five traits—avoiding conventions.

However, make an exception for ELLs and those with special needs. After they write an idea, make sure it's readable (conventions) before pushing them to write more (ideas).

Teacher Tip

Number the items on the "Done" list. Students note at the top of their drafts which revision tasks they applied. Monitor their revision choices. If necessary, cover up or remove the overused strategies forcing them to try new skills.

Follow-Up Lessons

Grow the "Done" List throughout the year. Add specific revision tasks based on new skills taught.

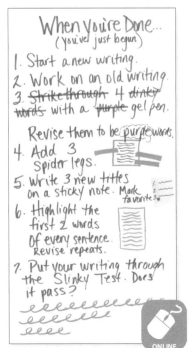

MINI-LESSON #2: Make space for revision

Revision shouldn't be about rewriting or recopying. Teach students ways to make room for additional information within a draft. They need space to add, change, and cut content without recopying any parts.

NOTE: Introduce one strategy per mini-lesson.

The **caret** is a simple way to insert 1-3 word details.

Don't erase. Simply **strikethrough**. It allows the reader to see the initial word choice and the revised synonyms.

Colored pens make revision more fun and more visible. It's easier to see the improvements students made.

Adding words or a single sentence on a **sticky note** can be more fun than just writing in the margins with a No. 2 pencil.

When the writer wants to move a sentence into a different position, the **circle & arrow** strategy is easy to follow.

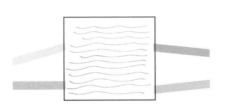

Add individual sentences using **spider legs**— each strip of paper (a "leg") is taped onto the "body" of the piece.

Story surgery cuts open the guts of the writing, adds a section, and tapes it back together. Think of it like inserting a new organ.

 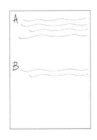

Create an **inserts page** as an alternative to story surgery. Using an endnote symbol within his draft, the writer indicates where he wants to add more. Then, using the same symbol on a second sheet of paper, he writes out the additional sentences.

Teacher Tip

For classrooms composing digitally, changing font colors reveals revisions made. Assign one color for revising verbs, another color to represent adding details, a third color for inserting transitions, etc.

Teacher Tip

Students need to make room for revision when working with a spiral notebook or marbled composition book. If they write only on the right-hand side of the page, they can return to a previous writing and use the left page for revising and editing.

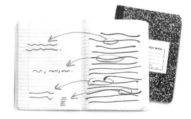

Teacher Tip

Some writers may not like all of these revision strategies. Explain that students can pick which revision techniques they like best once they have tried them all.

Independent Writing:

Students should revise a previous piece applying a revision strategy.

MINI-LESSON #3: Introduce Revision BINGO

When the "Done" list novelty wears off, try Revision BINGO. Following the principles of the game, writers apply any five consecutive revision strategies. (This includes horizontal, vertical, or diagonal. There is no "free" space.) This approach still allows the writer some choice and doesn't force him to improve everything.

Create a *Revision BINGO* chart. Incorporate 25 writing skills and strategies previously taught that students can apply independently. Remember, the strategies listed in each box should be task-specific and include a writing tool (Mini-Lesson #2, p. 33).

Teacher Tip

The strategies from the growing "Done" list first semester can become the strategies on *Revision BINGO* second semester. Be conscious to line up each five-box series so there is a mixture of easy and difficult strategies.

Teacher Tip

An editable *Revision BINGO* handout is available via the online resource. Tweak it to include only revision strategies and writing skills previously taught. Students cannot apply self-revision independently if they are unfamiliar with the skills or strategies.

Follow-Up Lesson

This lesson and resource is for *Revision BINGO*— tasks that target the traits of ideas, organization, voice, word choice, and sentence fluency. See Follow-Up Lesson on p. 37 for *Editing BINGO*, which targets convention corrections only.

ONLINE RESOURCE

Revision BINGO

Using your current writing, apply any five strategies in a row.
Indicate which ones you utilized by marking the boxes with an **X**.
When you've made the changes, staple this Bingo sheet to your writing.

Name _____

Add 3 emotionally charged words to your piece. **Voice**	Find a word, phrase, or sentence to cut. Strikethrough it with a purple pen. **Ideas**	Using a blue pen, add 3 number details (e.g., date, quantity, time, age, temperature, etc.). **Ideas**	Count the number of words per sentence; write the totals in the margins. Revise sentences that don't move the "Slinky." **Sentence Fluency**	Replace 3 generic nouns with more precise synonyms. **Word Choice**
Write/Rewrite a transition sentence to improve the flow from one paragraph to another. **Organization**	Insert words or phrases into a sentence to make it follow the rule of three. **Sentence Fluency**	Revise a sentence/ part for stronger voice and attitude. Mark the portion with an * asterisk. **Voice**	Find an idea to explain further by answering "why." **Ideas**	Use a blue pen to add a Show, Don't Tell section. **Voice/Word Choice**
Insert 4 specific name details (proper nouns). **Ideas**	Add prepositional phrases to three different sentences. **Sentence Fluency**	Circle 4 weak verbs. Replace them with strong action verbs. This may require rewriting the sentences. **Word Choice**	Write 3 optional titles on a sticky note. Circle your favorite. **Organization**	Add 2 similes and 1 metaphor. **Sentence Fluency**
Revise a sentence to include unique punctuation (e.g., parentheses, dashes, colons, ellipses etc.). **Sentence Fluency**	Insert 3 strong adverbs within your writing. **Word Choice**	Use the circle & arrow strategy to move around a sentence(s) to improve the order and flow of ideas. **Organization**	Write your intended attitude/tone at the top of your paper. Add 2 sentences to help convey that feeling. **Voice**	Rework a sentence to create an alliterative phrase. **Sentence Fluency**
Add sensory details in 2 different places within your writing. **Word Choice**	Write 2 new first-liners (hooks) on a sticky note. Circle your favorite. **Organization**	Highlight the first 2 words of every sentence in orange. Revise repeats. **Sentence Fluency**	Add 3 spider-leg sentences to your piece. **Ideas**	Clarify an idea by inserting a specific example. **Ideas**

Section 4: Motivating Writers
Mini-Lesson #3 — Introduce Revision BINGO

Launching the Writer's Workshop: Grades 3-12, Kristina Smekens & Maureen Scane
© 2017 Smekens Education Solutions, Inc.

Independent Writing:

Provide each student with a *Revision BINGO* handout. Have them apply five consecutive strategies to a previous writing. As they complete a revision task, they should mark off the box. Let students know that it might take more than one day to complete all five revision strategies. Students staple the Revision BINGO to their drafts when they turn them in.

MINI-LESSON #4: Develop productive peer conversations

Peer conferences often include one student telling another *I like your story. Your writing is good. I think you're done.* Combat this with four questions that result in specific peer feedback during a productive conversation.

1. **What's the best part?** *What's so good you wish you'd written it? What word, phrase, sentence, or part do you think the writer should leave alone because it's already good?* **Mark 1 best part.**

2. **What do you want more of?** *What did the writer start to mention but not give enough information about? What details should the writer add to his writing?* **Mark many add-more parts.**

3. **What's fuzzy?** *Are there any confusing parts? Is anything written in a weird or awkward way? Did you get lost?* **Mark any fuzzy parts.**

4. **What do you want less of?** *What word, idea, or phrase should the writer use less of? What parts are off-topic and need to be cut? Is there any part that moves too slowly and needs to be written more concisely?* **Mark at least 1 part/word to cut.**

My Teacher had a Rip in his Pants

Just about a week ago my teacher had a rip in his pants. It was really funny. I didn't see it right away but someone told me then I saw it and wanted to laugh but I held it in. Then someone told him and every start-ed to laugh. Then he went home to change

REVISED

A Kid's Dream Come True

Every kid has a dream that their teacher will disappear one day. Well, in our case, it finally came true.
Mr. Friedman was writing our math home-work on the board last Wednesday. The list was nger and longer, and finally, as he bent rite the last list of problems to do from textbook, his pants ripped—right in barrassing spot. We'd all noticed that were getting tighter and tighter over ew months, but none of us dreamed would finally just give up.
one started to laugh, and Mr. Friedman, turned, glared at us, grabbed at the rip and darted out of the room. It wasn't long before Mrs. Ahlery came in to finish up the class. She told us all to settle down and get back to work. I think she was trying to hold back a little giggle, but she never talked about what had happened. The good news is Mr. Friedman never did come back that afternoon.

Practice applying the four questions with an anchor paper. *Class, imagine you are the partner of the student who wrote the following piece* (e.g., "My Teacher Had a Rip in His Pants"). *When I'm done reading it aloud, we are going to give this author some feedback by answering the four revision questions.* Read the first draft, and then ask each revision question.

- *So what's the best part?* Listen to students' comments and then mark the single best part with a star using a green pen (to match the card).

- *What do you want to know more about?* Push students to identify all the details or sections that could be fleshed out. Identify questions the reader wants answers to. Mark them with plus signs (to match the card).

- *Is there anything fuzzy?* Ideas may be confusing because things are left out, or maybe there are parts that sound awkward based on their sentence structure. Mark any of them with a question mark using a red pen (to match the card).

- *Part of revision is removing weak parts. What word, detail, sentence, or part should be cut?* Mark it with a minus sign using a blue pen (to match the card).

Reveal the final draft of the anchor paper (e.g., "A Kid's Dream Come True") to note how the author addressed the students' questions.

Independent Writing:

Partners apply the Revision Conferencing Cards to a previous piece. When done, students revise independently.

MINI-LESSON #5: Read up and write down

Revision makes the piece *sound* better (Mini-Lessons #1 - #4, pp. 32-35); whereas, editing makes it *look* better. It's about fixing the conventions. Editing involves making the writing more correct. Writers check their spelling, punctuation, capitalization, spacing, paragraph indents, grammar, etc.

Writers edit for the reader's sake. In order to comprehend the writer's message, the reader expects certain rules to be followed. Not-even-close spelling makes the reader guess at words. Incorrect use of apostrophes makes the reader wonder who owns something. Missing end marks makes the reader stumble and reread.

However, the writer is so invested in the piece, he has a hard time looking at it objectively. Not to mention, if he *just* finished writing it, then it's hard to read it with fresh eyes. (Putting multiple days between the drafting and editing stages is best, but it's not always an option.) Increase the possibility of a writer catching his own mistakes with this 3-step process.

1. **Read Up, Write Down.** When a student writes, his paper is flat down on his desk. However, when editing, the student should turn into a reader by lifting his paper up off the writing surface. Thus, read "up" and write "down." By shifting from a writer's perspective to a reader's perspective, students edit more authentically.

   1. **LIFT** THE PAPER TO READ IT.
      Lay it down to make a change.
   2. **WHISPER** READ ALOUD.
      Move your lips!
   3. **TRACK** THE WORDS.
      Touch them when you read

   ONLINE RESOURCE

2. **Whisper read.** No one reads as fast out loud as he does silently. Therefore, writers should reread their pieces aloud. Their lips should physically move during a whisper reading. This will slow down the students. (NOTE: Don't let students slide back into a silent reading after a few sentences of whisper reading.)

3. **Follow with finger.** As they whisper read, students should track each word with their index fingers. Sometimes a writer thinks he wrote a word, but the word never made it onto the paper; his brain was moving faster than his pencil.

Have students pull out an old draft and practice the *Read-Up, Write-Down* steps. Monitor that their lips are actually moving. Encourage them to track each word, bouncing their fingers across the page, rather than sliding over the words. Remind students that when they find errors, they should turn back into writers by laying the piece down on the desk and making the changes. Then they lift, whisper, and track to resume the "read up" editing position.

Independent Writing:

Students self-edit previous writings applying the three steps of *Read Up, Write Down*. During Author's Chair, have students report how many mistakes they found and fixed in their own drafts. Celebrate that they were successful editors of their own writing!

Teacher Tip

These steps apply to composing on the computer, too. Rather than just editing off the screen, students should print a hard copy. Although written at a 90-degree plane (the computer screen), it's edited at a 45-degree reader's plane. This shift is apt to cause the students to find more mistakes.

Teacher Tip

To make whisper reading more fun, utilize a whisper phone. Made from curved PVC piping pieces or purchased from a teacher store, these phones make it more fun to read aloud.

Teacher Tip

Consider creating a building-wide set of proofreading marks. If teachers and students *all* utilized the same set, then self-editing, peer-editing, and teacher-editing would be more efficient and consistent.

Launching the Writer's Workshop: Grades 3-12, Kristina Smekens and Maureen Scane
© 2017 Smekens Education Solutions, Inc.

MINI-LESSON #6: Conduct focused edits

Editing one's own work is often a difficult task, as everything makes sense to the person who wrote it. For others, the editing process is overwhelming when it's accompanied by a lengthy checklist of skills to look for.

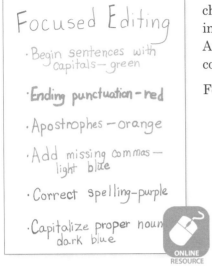

Focused Editing
· Begin sentences with capitals—green
· Ending punctuation—red
· Apostrophes—orange
· Add missing commas—light blue
· Correct spelling—purple
· Capitalize proper noun dark blue

Rather than providing a self-editing checklist, conduct focused editing. This includes zeroing in on one skill at a time. And if each skill is edited with a different color pen, it's just more fun.

For example:
- **Read once** for beginning-sentence and proper noun capitals with a green pen.
- Then read the piece for a **second time** and edit in red for missing or incorrect end punctuation (.!?).
- Read the writing a **third time** correcting apostrophes (both possessives and contractions) with an orange pen.

Identify the first skills for all students to edit for (e.g., capitals, end punctuation, paragraph indents). Assign a color to each skill. Begin a "Focused Editing" wall chart that includes these convention skills and their corresponding editing pen colors.

While students are conducting the edit, make sure they are also applying the *Read-Up, Write-Down* strategy (Mini-Lesson #5, p. 36). Students should apply the three steps to *every* focused edit.

Independent Writing:

Students reread a previous draft multiple times. During each reading, the writer focuses on a different skill using the designated pen colors.

Teacher Tip

Store the editing pens in a single location within the classroom. Introduce a new area to the writing environment (the Editing Station).

Teacher Tip

Grow the "Focused Editing" list just like the "Done" list (Follow-Up Lesson on p. 32). After teaching additional convention skills, add them to the wall chart.

Differentiate the editing expectations. Struggling writers should continue to edit for basic sentence-writing conventions while high-ability writers are ready for more sophisticated convention skills. For more information on this procedure, watch "Conduct Focused Edits" via the online resource.

Follow-Up Lessons

The strategies from the growing "Focused Editing" list first semester can become the strategies on *Editing BINGO* second semester. Be conscious to line up each five-box series so there is a mixture of easy and difficult convention strategies.

Adjust the writing process

Much of writing instruction includes teaching writing skills within the writing process. The traits live within the stages of the writing process.

STEP 1: PRE-WRITE	Writers create a plan identifying the information and details they want to include and the order they want to reveal them.	**THINK UP** the ideas and organization appropriate for the audience (i.e., voice).
STEP 2: DRAFT	Whether handwriting or typing the piece, writers compose a first draft.	**WRITE UP** the details (ideas) in order (organization), fleshing out each idea into sentences.
STEP 3: REVISE	Add information, delete the irrelevant, rearrange the organization, replace weak words, and polish sentence structure.	**DOCTOR UP** the ideas, organization, voice, word choice, and sentence fluency.
STEP 4: EDIT	With the message complete, writers correct it for grammar and mechanics.	**FIX UP** the conventions.
STEP 5: PUBLISH	Writing is meant to be shared with its intended audience. It's no longer just for the writer's eyes, but now for a reader's.	Present the piece or **PUT IT UP** via uploading, posting, sharing, or putting it away.

The standards state that students should experience the writing process in long, extended *and* short, compressed time frames. The latter requires teachers to create opportunities for students to start and finish a piece in one sitting. This mirrors the real world; rarely are individuals producing writings they have crafted across multiple days.

The teacher must show students how to adjust the pacing of the writing process based on the task and circumstance. Different writing scenarios allow for more or less time. For example, they can take days to pre-write and draft a three-week research paper, but they have less than an hour to pre-write and draft a response on a standardized writing assessment.

STEPS 3 & 4: CHECK & CHANGE	When time and space are limited, writers make minor improvements to the first draft before publishing it (Step 5).	**SPEED UP** revision and editing with minor changes to ideas, word choice, & conventions.

These faster experiences still utilize the steps of the writing process. Writers still pre-write and draft, they just have less time to do them. In addition, rather than a full-out revision or perfected edit, they conduct a quick check and make minor changes (e.g., insertion of details, substitution of word choices, quick convention fixes, etc.). Within a one-sitting writing, students don't have the luxury of time (multiple days), resources (peer support), or space (first draft only). This is the writing process done in minutes, rather than across days.

Visual Triggers

Utilize these mini-posters to define the purpose of each step of the writing process.

For downloadable mini-posters, read "Seeing the Traits within the Writing Process" via the online resource.

Teacher Tip

There is a definitive difference between revision and editing. For more information on the skills and traits involved, see "Understanding the Difference Between Revision and Editing" via the online resource.

Teacher Tip

Train students to work within time constraints using a time management system. Customize a variety of options available via the online resource.

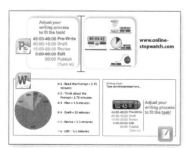

Launching the Writer's Workshop: Grades 3-12, Kristina Smekens and Maureen Scane
© 2017 Smekens Education Solutions, Inc.

Targeting Spelling

SECTION 5

Teachers should not spell words for students during writing time. Writing expert Ralph Fletcher says that feeds the *writer's welfare* system. Students become dependent on others for word spellings and eventually expect that level of support constantly.

Therefore, outline expectations for how students should handle spelling needs. Looking words up in the dictionary is a necessary action when focusing on editing and conventions in a final draft. However, telling them to look up all unknown words in the dictionary is not necessarily an appropriate first-draft (or standardized-assessment-appropriate) spelling strategy.

Consequently, students need first-draft spelling strategies that they can employ independently and efficiently.

Procedural Mini-Lessons

MINI-LESSON #1: Develop independent spellers

Equip students to be independent first-draft spellers. Brainstorm writer strategies that reveal what students can do when they do not know how to spell a word. The list might include:

- Sound out the word.
- Ask a peer for help.
- Look around the room. The word may be on the wall.
- Look for the word on a related handout/book page.
- Think of a rhyming word. Spell it similarly.
- Write out the word parts you know (prefix, suffix, root, etc.).
- Draw a rebus/simple picture as a placeholder (☂ = umbrella).
- Try your best and mark it with a squiggle line (e.g., kunkushin).

Conclude the lesson noting that none of the strategies on the poster include "Ask the teacher." Clarify that the teacher does not spell words for writers. Rather, students should utilize various first-draft strategies to approximate the spellings.

Independent Writing:

Students write a new first draft. Encourage them to utilize some on-the-spot spelling strategies. Then later, when editing, they can pour over the spelling. (During Author's Chair, ask students which spelling strategies they found themselves utilizing.)

Teacher Tip

Initially, brainstorm a couple of grade-appropriate spelling strategies for the wall chart. Then, "grow" it as the year progresses and new skills are taught.

Teacher Tip

Misspellings in digital documents are indicated by a red squiggle line below the word. Consequently, don't tell students to circle words they are unsure about. Rather, have them utilize the universal symbol they will see forevermore— the squiggle line.

Teacher Tip

Most standardized writing assessment rubrics honor "bigger" more precise words that may be spelled wrong over little, overused words spelled correctly. Encourage students to be spelling risk-takers and to go for the more precise word choice, even if they are unsure of the exact spelling.

Teacher Tip

Although using a dictionary may not be an appropriate *first*-draft spelling strategy, students must make this tool part of their more formal editing process.

MINI-LESSON #2: Check squiggle-line spellings

Simply marking a questionable word spelling with a squiggle line is *not* enough. There is a second step to that strategy; eventually writers actually look the word up in the dictionary.

The purpose behind the squiggle line is only to make it easier to locate the questionable word later. The squiggle line is not an "out," giving kids permission to use whatever spelling they want.

Review resources within the room where students can go to look up word spellings (e.g., dictionaries, computerized spell check, word charts, etc.). Model how to strikethrough the original word within the draft and write the correct spelling above it.

Independent Writing:

Return to previous pieces that students marked unsure words with squiggle lines. Have them use classroom resources to verify or fix spellings.

Launching the Writer's Workshop: Grades 3-12, Kristina Smekens and Maureen Scane
© 2017 Smekens Education Solutions, Inc.

MINI-LESSON #3: Provide topic-driven word charts

Support students' spelling needs and build their independence with word charts. Each picture-based word chart can be printed, laminated, and made accessible for students during writing time.

 Nearly 30 pre-made word charts are accessible via the online resource. Each is an editable Word document, allowing teachers to add or replace clip-art images as appropriate.

Create additional word charts for student interests, science/social studies content, field trips and school events, etc.

Begin a first draft on a topic with which students are very familiar. While writing, use a precise word but pretend not to know how to spell it. Model the strategy of using the topic-related word chart to acquire the correct spelling.

Through the modeling process, demonstrate:
- Where the word charts are stored.
- How to utilize the images to quickly find the word.
- How to transfer the spelling from the word chart to the draft.
- How to return the word chart so it's available for others to use.

Reveal 3-5 word charts. Go over the words/images per topic. Then add the laminated charts to the classroom environment.

Independent Writing:

Encourage students to utilize their independent spelling strategies (Mini-Lesson #1, p. 40) and these word charts during writing time.

Teacher Tip

Because of the corresponding picture support, word charts are a fabulous resource for ELL and special needs students.

Teacher Tip

Initially, introduce a couple of word charts on topics students are writing about regularly. Slowly add a chart or two to the resource each week. If *all* the word charts are available right away, students tend to forget they exist. However, a slow growing resource keeps it in the front of their minds.

Follow-Up Lessons

Photocopy a popular word chart that many students might need at the same time (e.g., Christmas/holiday words). Provide each student a personal copy to use at his desk and store within his writer's notebook.

MINI-LESSON #4: Require a *You do, I do* attitude

You do, I do is a strategy that offers students *some* teacher support, while still nudging them to become spelling risk-takers.

When a student wants a word spelled for him, he must first attempt the word on paper all by himself. Then, below his attempt, the teacher writes the correct spelling. Point out the phonics and spelling rules the student applied accurately. Target the sounds he confused or misused.

The advantage to this procedure is that the writer gets what he ultimately wanted— the correct word spelling. But the teacher required him to first use independent strategies in order to earn that extra spelling support.

Independent Writing:

During writing time, encourage students to be spelling risk-takers, while offering the *You do, I do* approach as students request it.

Teacher Tip

This spelling strategy is a fabulous resource for ELL and special needs students.

Teacher Tip

This procedure works in conjunction with the Help! Tent/Strip (Mini-Lesson #5, p. 25). After a writer has done the *You do* on a sticky note, then he adheres it to his Help! Tent/Strip. That signals to the teacher that he is ready for help (*I do*). The teacher writes the correct spelling on the sticky note. The students applies the spelling to his piece and then sticks the note within the "Helpful Hints" section (p. 29) of his notebook for future reference.

MINI-LESSON #5: Define convention formality

The die-hard grammarian wants to take points off for students who write: *ur* (your), *2moro* (tomorrow), *btw* (by the way), or *l8r* (later) in any assignment. A teacher's first instinct may be to claim text-message spelling is *wrong*.

However, within the texting genre, those *are* the appropriate spelling conventions. (In fact anyone who spells every word correctly and punctuates and capitalizes every text-message sentence is breaking the rules of the texting genre!) That said, this mini-lesson is not about right or wrong spelling, as much as appropriateness. Depending on the purpose, audience, and genre, there are different levels of convention formality to adhere to.

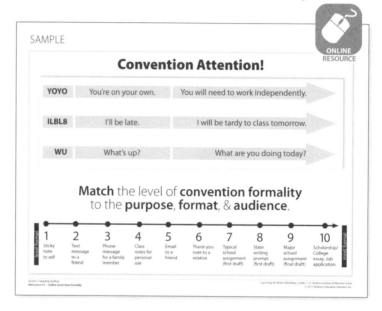

Draw a long horizontal line on the board. Label the far left as "least formal" (level 1) and the far right as "most formal" (level 10). Discuss the different types of writing that exist. Slowly plot them on the spectrum based on their convention formality. For example:

- School-assignment writing poses higher convention standards than a text message to a peer or a note passed to a friend.
- Poetry has lower convention expectations than an essay on a standardized writing assessment.
- A final draft should be more correct and more formal, than a first draft.

Independent Writing:

Announce a writing topic for students to respond to (e.g., fabricate a food fight that happened on the previous day). Have students handwrite a text message to a friend who was absent. They are to give all the details using texting conventions (or lack thereof).

Then, have students write to the same topic, but this time their audience is the school principal. The principal needs documentation of the incident from each of them, as they were eyewitnesses. With a different purpose and audience, the students' spelling and conventions change.

Discuss the students' convention choices between the two pieces.

Teacher Tip

Students' cell phone use is increasing. And all that text messaging has impacted the spelling within classroom writing assignments. Address this issue with a mini-lesson early in the year.

Visual Triggers

Compare this concept to various levels of dress. Pajamas and sweatpants are comfortable loungewear but not appropriate for the formal setting of a wedding. It's all about appropriateness.

Teacher Tip

This concept of a 1-10 formality range may be a conversation to have as an entire building/department/grade-level team. Consistent expectations within all subject-area writing helps students master this skill sooner.

Teacher Tip

If possible, project the students' writings during Author's Chair. The convention conversation is best when students can see each other's spellings.

Launching the Writer's Workshop: Grades 3-12, Kristina Smekens and Maureen Scane
© 2017 Smekens Education Solutions, Inc.

Introducing the Traits

SECTION 6

Sections 1-5 define good *writer* habits. Section 6 defines good *writing*.

According to research, the six ingredients within all modes, genres, and formats of writing are ideas, organization, voice, word choice, sentence fluency, and conventions. These are the 6 Traits!

To be most effective, teachers and students need to have a common language to describe good writing. Without a definition, students are forever asking *Is this good? Am I done? Is this what you want?*

Plan an annual introduction (or re-introduction) of the 6-Traits terminology early in the school year. Then, kick off every writing lesson identifying the trait it supports. Students slowly learn the small sub-skills that comprise each trait. Rather than thinking about dozens of individual and isolated skills they have to execute, students compartmentalize them into the six trait categories.

Instructional Insights

Trait-Introduction Mini-Lessons

Teacher Tip

Find out how much trait exposure students had in previous grades. This will help determine how fast this year's introduction/*re*-introduction should move as well as revealing what strategies to avoid repeating.

Introduce each trait— The Mini-Lesson

An intentional 6-Traits introduction should be conducted every year as a means of establishing common language in the writing classroom. Some introductions occur over a few days, others require numerous mini-lessons. Choose the most appropriate strategy depending on the students' grade level and prior trait knowledge.

Because the 6 Traits are not a program, there is no *one* way to introduce the traits to students. However, there do seem to be three common principles guiding the strongest trait-based classrooms.

1. **Present the traits efficiently.** Roll them out within consecutive mini-lessons. The goal is that students realize how these six ingredients work together.

2. **Provide an overview of the traits.** This introduction is simply to *expose* students to each trait and its general definition. Students will *not* yet apply the traits proficiently within their own writing.

3. **Introduce the traits uniformly.** Utilize a common approach for all six traits. The four options within this section (Mini-Lessons #1 - #4, pp. 46-49) outline classroom-tested strategies for introducing the 6 Traits.

Typically, a trait introduction would consume six mini-lessons— one per trait.

DAY 1	DAY 2	DAY 3	DAY 4	DAY 5	DAY 6
Ideas	Organization	Voice	Word Choice	Sent. Fluency	Conventions

A slower trait introduction is ideal for intermediate writers (grades 3-5) and/or those who have had no exposure to the traits in previous years. This would likely include two mini-lessons per trait.

DAYS 1-2	DAYS 3-4	DAYS 5-6	DAYS 7-8	DAYS 9-10	DAYS 11-12
Ideas	Organization	Voice	Word Choice	Sent. Fluency	Conventions

If students have had a lot of experience with the traits in previous grade levels, then a faster *re*-introduction works well. Review two traits per mini-lesson, showing students how they impact one another.

DAY 1	DAY 2	DAY 3
Ideas & Organization	Voice & Word Choice	Sent. Fluency & Conventions

Secondary teachers inheriting students who have a deep understanding of the traits may conduct a one-day rapid review (Mini-Lesson #4, p. 49).

DAY 1
Ideas, Organization, Voice, Word Choice, Sent. Fluency, & Conventions

Launching the Writer's Workshop: Grades 3-12, Kristina Smekens and Maureen Scane
© 2017 Smekens Education Solutions, Inc.

Experiment with each trait— The Writing Time

The writer's workshop *always* includes a writing time after the mini-lesson— even on these trait-introduction days. However, the lesson wasn't focused on *how* to write with a trait as much as defining *what* the trait looks like. Therefore, after a mini-lesson that identifies a trait, provide an opportunity to experiment with the trait in a quick write.

The key to a successful writing time on these days is choosing a topic that lends itself to playing with a particular trait. If students are to dabble with voice, identify an emotional topic. If students are to focus on sequential organization, then choose a chronological subject. Here are suggested writing-time topics to follow the introductory mini-lessons.

- **Ideas:** *Write about a topic you know a lot about. Choose a topic you are an "expert" on and write with as much detail as possible.*

- **Organization:** *Reflect on what you did from the moment you woke up until you were seated at your desk at school this morning. Walk the reader through your morning moment by moment.*

- **Voice:** *Voice requires emotion. So, think about an event or memory that made you especially happy, sad, or mad. Label the top of your quick write with the feeling you are trying to convey. Then attempt to convey that emotion without ever using that word (or a synonym).*

- **Word Choice:** *Write about a particular place or a specialized skill. Be conscious of the vocabulary an expert on this topic would use. Attempt to write with vivid adjectives, precise nouns, and action verbs.*

- **Sentence Fluency:** *Reread the pieces you've written during these trait introduction days (i.e., ideas, organization, voice, word choice). Identify long sentences and short sentences and middle-length sentences you've written. Determine if you have a good mixture— or are they all about the same length? Can you make some changes to improve the sentence fluency?*

- **Conventions:** *Now that we know conventions are for the reader, self-edit to make your writing more clear for the reader. Reread the drafts you've written over the past five days, editing for spelling, punctuation, capitalization, grammar, etc.*

Teacher Tip

Students will produce quick writes each day. These are in-class writings that simply provide a chance to play with a trait. Don't plan to grade them, but do save and store them within the "Abandoned Writing" section of their writer's notebooks (p. 29).

Teacher Tip

If each trait introduction spans two mini-lessons, then it requires two different writing-time topics. For example, following the first mini-lesson introducing Organization, students can write about getting ready for school. The second day, they can write about getting ready for bed.

Mini-Lesson Series #1: Define each trait visually & verbally

Define each trait with a simple definition. Reveal the function the trait serves within the writing. However, keep the explanation general during the introduction. The rest of the year is devoted to digging into the traits via mini-lessons and writing application.

In addition, provide a visual trigger to anchor the trait's meaning.

Teacher Tip

With consistent visual icons, students hear the same trait words from year to year and see the same graphics. This develops building-wide consistency in imple-mentation and writing expectations. Smekens Education icons are all available via the online resource.

Purchase the *Let Your Voice Be Heard* poster or cre-ate one with students' faces.

Substitute a smart phone for the whisper phone and/ or a tool belt for the tool box.

DAY 1
Ideas

Definition: The main idea, message, what the writing is all about.
Icon: light bulb

The light bulb represents the topic or idea. It can also be compared to a dimmer switch. The brightness of the light parallels the devel-opment of reasons, examples, and support. Short writing reflects dim ideas; developed writing represents bright ideas.

DAY 2
Organization

Definition: The logical order of information.
Icon: train

The train reminds students that cohesive writing always has three parts— an introduction, a body, and a conclusion. The ideas within each part (or train car) are all hitched together or connected with transitions.

DAY 3
Voice

Definition: The writer's attitude or feeling about the topic.
Icon: faces/facial expressions

Voice or tone is based on the writer's attitude about his writing topic, and facial expressions depict those same emotions.

DAY 4
Word Choice

Definition: The use of specific and precise bullseye vocabulary.
Icon: bullseye board/target

Specific word choice comes down to bullseye writing. The center identifies specific and precise word choice —versus vague and gen-eral words that miss the mark.

DAY 5
Sentence Fluency

Definition: The smooth rhythm and flow of sentences.
Icon: whisper phone/smart phone

Sentence fluency is an auditory trait. It is the ease and readability of a piece. Writers read aloud their pieces to check that they sound good and sound right.

DAY 6
Conventions

Definition: The level of correctness.
Icon: tool box/tool belt

Writers utilize tools from the conventions tool box/tool belt to help the reader. These "tools" include capitalization, spelling, punctua-tion, grammar, paragraph indents, etc.

Independent Writing:

Students experiment with each trait following the mini-lesson. See p. 45 for suggested writing-time tasks.

Mini-Lesson Series #2: Reveal mentor text examples

Define each trait with a simple one-sentence explanation (Mini-Lesson #1, p. 46). Then show an example of it in action. This is the concept of mentor text. During the lesson, the teacher would read aloud the text, pausing to point out different places where that trait is evident. Don't expect students to participate much in the lesson. They are listening to the text and taking in the comments the teacher is making about it. Remember, this is likely their first exposure to the trait. Students need the teacher to point it out in action.

Picture books are a popular choice of mentor text, however, don't feel limited to the suggested titles. The traits are in *all* writing. Consequently, any text that exemplifies the trait would be fine, including informational text or everyday, real-world examples (e.g., newspaper articles, comic strips, text messages, billboards, online articles, etc.).

Teacher Tip

For current grade-level suggestions, see "Kristina's Favorite Picture Books for Teaching the 6 Traits" via the online resource.

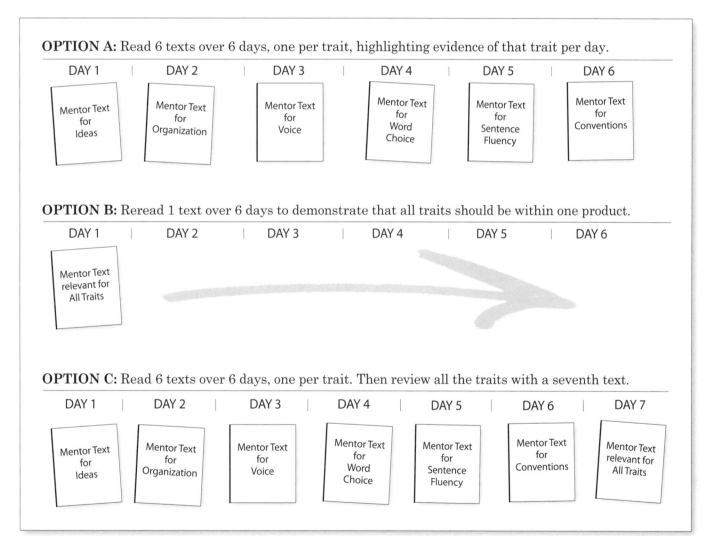

OPTION A: Read 6 texts over 6 days, one per trait, highlighting evidence of that trait per day.

DAY 1	DAY 2	DAY 3	DAY 4	DAY 5	DAY 6
Mentor Text for Ideas	Mentor Text for Organization	Mentor Text for Voice	Mentor Text for Word Choice	Mentor Text for Sentence Fluency	Mentor Text for Conventions

OPTION B: Reread 1 text over 6 days to demonstrate that all traits should be within one product.

DAY 1	DAY 2	DAY 3	DAY 4	DAY 5	DAY 6
Mentor Text relevant for All Traits					

OPTION C: Read 6 texts over 6 days, one per trait. Then review all the traits with a seventh text.

DAY 1	DAY 2	DAY 3	DAY 4	DAY 5	DAY 6	DAY 7
Mentor Text for Ideas	Mentor Text for Organization	Mentor Text for Voice	Mentor Text for Word Choice	Mentor Text for Sentence Fluency	Mentor Text for Conventions	Mentor Text relevant for All Traits

Independent Writing:

Students experiment with each trait following the mini-lesson. See p. 45 for suggested writing-time tasks.

Video Clips

Access six videos of students performing a song per trait. Watch "6-Traits Song Upgrade" via the online resource.

Teacher Tip

Add the song lyrics to the yearlong display (p. 50), as some students will remember a trait's meaning because of the tune stuck in their heads.

Mini-Lesson Series #3: Sing trait-based songs

Music is a powerful learning style for many students. It's memorable both in its catchy lyrics but also in its rhythm and beat. Consequently, finding a way to tie the trait introduction to music is a worthwhile approach.

There are various 6-Traits songs out there, although many are tied to nursery rhyme tunes like "Row, Row, Row Your Boat" or "Mary Had a Little Lamb." Consider the chorus of current/popular songs that students are familiar with. Now imagine the lyrics revised to reveal the meaning of a writing trait. Many creative teachers have tried this and shared their customized lyrics (see Video Clips to the left).

The key to a powerful trait introduction is that students understand each trait's meaning and its function in good writing based on the lyrics themselves. Consequently, spend the mini-lesson time pouring over each song's trait-based lyrics. Dissect what it reveals about the trait. Make comparisons and connections to writing skills students have background knowledge about. Even identify some of the new skills noted in the lyrics that students will learn throughout the year.

OPTION A: Introduce each trait with song lyrics that define its meaning.					
DAY 1	**DAY 2**	**DAY 3**	**DAY 4**	**DAY 5**	**DAY 6**
Ideas Song	Organization Song	Voice Song	Word Choice Song	Sent. Fluency Song	Conventions Song

For a slower and more in-depth trait introduction, merge the mentor text examples (Mini-Lesson #2, p. 47) and this song approach to create a two-day-per-trait introduction.

OPTION B: Introduce each trait in a two-day pattern.					
Ideas	Organization	Voice	Word Choice	Sent. Fluency	Conventions
DAY 1: Text	**DAY 3:** Text	**DAY 5:** Text	**DAY 7:** Text	**DAY 9:** Text	**DAY 11:** Text
DAY 2: Song	**DAY 4:** Song	**DAY 6:** Song	**DAY 8:** Song	**DAY 10:** Song	**DAY 12:** Song

Independent Writing:

Students experiment with each trait following the mini-lesson. See p. 45 for suggested writing-time tasks.

Mini-Lesson Series #4: Conduct a one-day rapid review

Secondary teachers inheriting students who have a *deep* understanding of the traits may conduct a one-day rapid review. However, don't dismiss a trait *re*introduction altogether. Students who are veterans to the traits need to know this year's teacher utilizes the language, too. Students new to the district need a crash course in the language writers are expected to use. And those students who are not new, but who haven't been very attentive, typically need a reminder.

Plan a single day to review all 6 traits.

- Facilitate a short discussion about the traits. Inquire about what students remember about each one. See if they can recall the visual icons, picture books, or song lyrics from previous years.
- Put students in one of six groups and provide them markers and chart paper.
- Assign each group a trait to label at the top of their chart paper.
- Give them approximately 10 minutes to generate a group poster for their trait that includes everything that group of students remembers about the trait. Suggest students provide a definition, list relevant sub-skills, draw the icon, note any mentor text titles, write out the song lyrics, etc.
- After the allotted time, have students *leave* their posters, get up, and carousel to a different trait poster.
- They will read the poster, discuss what they think the previous group meant, confirm their understanding of the trait, and add any new information to make the poster more representative of the trait.
- Students continue to carousel until every group has read every trait poster.

Teacher Tip

Teachers would only utilize this mini-lesson *if* students can recall several things about each trait. They can't just know *of* the traits; students need to know them deeply. (If they do not, utilize strategies from Mini-Lessons #1-#3, pp. 46-48 to conduct a deliberate trait introduction.)

Teacher Tip

For those who teach multiple periods, plan to execute this activity within all of your ELA classes. The following day, have each class vote on the "best" Ideas poster, Organization poster, Voice poster, etc. The "winning" posters (one per trait) will remain as the yearlong display for all classes/sections (p. 50). The others will be discarded. As additional skills are taught, add them to these kid-made posters.

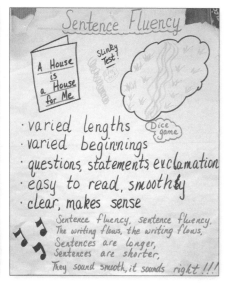

Independent Writing:

Groups will each present their posters. Inquire about what they wrote/drew, what it symbolizes, and how it fits the trait. Clarify what the group put on the poster and then what was added. Use this time to assess the students' understanding.

Teacher Tip

Be prepared to clarify misconceptions, misunderstandings, or inaccurate information about the traits. Some minor revisions might need to be made to the posters.

Teacher Tip

See dozens of 6-Trait displays at "Yearlong 6-Traits Bulletin Boards" via the online resource.

Represent the traits within the classroom environment

The 6 Traits are the core of all writing instruction; they anchor all mini-lessons. That said, consider their physical presence within the classroom. This visual display becomes a yearlong record of all the skills taught.

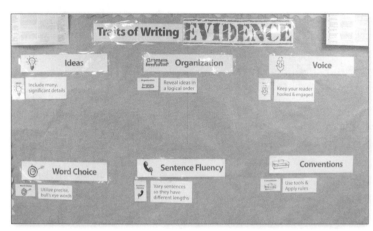

TRAIT EVIDENCE: A "themeless" display can include six sections— one per trait. Simply label each portion and add the icon during the introduction. The rest of the year, add the bulleted skills that encompass each trait.

LET IT RAIN GOOD WRITING: Initially, trait umbrellas went up along *with* picture book covers read during the introduction. Then, raindrop skills were added for specific mini-lessons.

SLAM DUNK YOUR WRITING: Backboards represented each trait. Basketballs identify specific skills learned throughout the year.

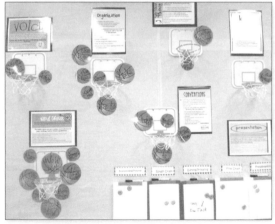

TREE OF GOOD WRITING: No spare bulletin board? No problem. Utilize chart paper. Introduce the traits with the six branches of good writing. Then add leaf skills per trait. NOTE: Another creative option is to use a portable science-fair presentation board and sticky notes.

TOYS & TRIGGERS: This display showcases the 6-Trait icons and various toys and triggers used to teach the traits all year long. It's also atop the bookshelf that holds the mentor text picture books the teacher references in writing mini-lessons.

ROCK-STAR WRITING: Guitars went up with each trait introduced. Then, musical notes identified specific skills.

Launching the Writer's Workshop: Grades 3-12, Kristina Smekens and Maureen Scane
© 2017 Smekens Education Solutions, Inc.

Building Rubrics

The building of the all-class writing rubric is the grand finale of the 6-Traits introduction. With common language between teacher and students to describe "good" writing in place, use it to create an assessment tool. It's not helpful to know the traits if they are not part of the self-, peer-, and teacher-assessment process.

The initial rubric will be skimpy and based on students' minimal knowledge of each trait. However, as new skills are taught, the teacher will up the ante of the rubric. An instructional classroom rubric grows with the students.

Procedural Mini-Lessons

#1 pp. 52-53   Define "rubric"
#2 pp. 54-55   Establish an initial writing rubric
#3 p. 56   Update the rubric frequently

Instructional Insights

p. 57   Utilize one rubric for all writing units
p. 57   Utilize one rubric for multiple grade levels
p. 58   Assess the relevant traits
p. 58   Provide feedback to students
p. 58   Convert rubric scores to grades

Launching the Writer's Workshop: Grades 3-12, Kristina Smekens and Maureen Scane
© 2017 Smekens Education Solutions, Inc.

51

MINI-LESSON #1: Define "rubric"

Before jumping in and creating a writing rubric, spend time defining the concept of a rubric.

Introduce the term *rubric* as a tool for grading, scoring, or assessing how good something is. A rubric describes the strengths of something and indicates what needs improvement.

Build a "Clean Desk" or "Clean Locker" rubric. Start with the highest level. Suggest the "traits" or categories of such a rubric. Provide a list of traits and ask students to describe what each would look like in a "clean" desk/locker. Jot down their descriptions.

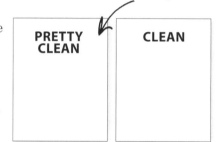

Traits for a CLEAN DESK	Traits for a CLEAN LOCKER
Books	Books
Folders	Trash
Trash	Coats/Clothing
Pencil box/School supplies	Odor

Then, add a second chart to the left of "Clean" and label it "Pretty Clean." Students again describe the same traits for this level. (Rubrics describe the same trait categories at every level.)

Add one more chart to represent the lowest level of the rubric. Don't label it "Messy," as that implies a negative connotation. Rather, label it something more neutral (e.g., "Time to Clean"). Repeat the process of jotting down the students' descriptions.

Identify each level with a number— Clean = Level 5, Pretty Clean = Level 3, Time to Clean = Level 1. Explain that it's possible to earn a Level 2 or Level 4. This happens when the desk/locker possesses some characteristics described in two different levels. (NOTE: Add in the two extra columns, but do NOT write any additional rubric criteria.)

Independent Writing:

As a class, assess a couple of desks/lockers. Using the rubric language, help students answer these three questions about each desk/locker:

- *What score does this desk/locker earn? Which level is it most like?*
- *Why is that score appropriate?* (Justify it with criteria from the rubric.)
- *What needs to be "revised" in the desk/locker to up its score?*

Teacher Tip

If students do not understand the fundamentals of a rubric (e.g., levels, traits, criteria, etc.), then execute this first mini-lesson. Students cannot build a writing rubric (Mini-Lesson #2, p. 54) if they don't even know what a rubric is.

Teacher Tip

While building the desk rubric, elementary students will most likely attempt to tidy their desks. However, a key component is self-assessment. So, prohibit students from reaching into their desks to clean. Consider having them turn their desks around, so that they can't access the insides.

Teacher Tip

The power in making kid-friendly rubrics with students is that they understand the criteria. This makes it possible for students to then apply the rubric in self- and peer-assessment.

Launching the Writer's Workshop: Grades 3-12, Kristina Smekens and Maureen Scane
© 2017 Smekens Education Solutions, Inc.

View example kid-friendly rubrics

1

TIME TO CLEAN
- Books are unorganized
- Pens/Pencils are out
- Papers are all over (sticking out)
- Papers and things hanging out of desk
- Trash in desk
- Folders and workbooks are crammed in desk

2

3

PRETTY CLEAN
- Some books organized
- Pencils/pens are mostly put up/in pencil holder
- No papers out in desk
- No trash
- Folders/workbooks are not together

4

5

CLEAN DESK
- Books Organized - books facing up
- No pencils/pens out
- No papers in desk
- No trash
- Folders + workbooks are together

Teacher Tip

The Clean Desk and Clean Locker Rubrics are holistic. They produce a single overall score of a Level 1, 2, 3, 4, or 5 based on the overall status of the desk or locker. However, a rubric is most useful when each trait (e.g., books, trash, folders, etc.) can be scored individually. This is called *analytic* scoring because the scorer can *analyze* each trait.

Teacher Tip

Including photos of desks/lockers at the various levels helps visual learners more accurately interpret criteria for the different levels.

ONLINE RESOURCES

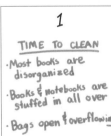

1

TIME TO CLEAN
- Most books are disorganized
- Books & notebooks are stuffed in all over
- Bags open & overflowing
- Several loose papers
- Cluttered / too full

2

3

PRETTY CLEAN LOCKER
- Some book spines face out - some are backwards
- A few books & notebooks in more than one place
- Some bags closed & hung up
- A few loose papers
- A little cluttered

4

5

CLEAN LOCKER
- All book spines face out
- All books & notebooks in one place
- One bag closed & hung up
- No loose papers
- No extra clutter

Teacher Tip

Identify three students' lockers to assess using the class-created Locker Rubric. Walk the entire class to each locker and apply the rubric. (If students take photos of the rubric they made in the classroom with their cell phones, then they can have the criteria with them for scoring.)

MINI-LESSON #2: Establish an initial writing rubric

Build a basic writing rubric utilizing the same process outlined in Mini-Lesson #1, pp. 52-53.

- Identify the traits of a writing rubric.
- Ask students to describe each trait at the highest level (e.g., "Great Writing"). Jot down their kid-friendly language.
- Add a second chart to the left of "Great Writing;" label it "Good Writing." Students again describe the specific criteria per trait within this level.
- Add a third chart to represent the lowest level of the rubric. Label it "Just Started Writing." This doesn't have the negative connotation of "Bad Writing" but clearly indicates it's a work in progress.
- Again, include parallel criteria per trait. (Skills listed in the highest level must be referenced within the lower levels, too.)
- Label the levels 1-5, reiterating that pieces earn a level 2 or level 4 when it has some characteristics from multiple levels.

Traits for a WRITING RUBRIC

Ideas
Organization
Voice
Word Choice
Sentence Fluency
Conventions

Independent Writing:

Reveal a writing sample to the class. Looking across each trait row, determine the individual trait scores for this piece. (Remind students that Levels 2 and 4 are options, too.)

- *What rubric level best represents the ideas in this piece?*
- *What level is the trait of organization most like?*
- *How would you score the voice in this piece?*
- *What score would it earn for word choice?*
- *Looking at the sentence fluency in the writing, what level is it most like?*
- *How would you rate the conventions?*

Ask students what the writer would have to do to improve the piece.
- *What revisions would he need to make in order to up his scores?*

After using the rubric, it's likely that some of the criteria may need to be clarified. Make revisions as needed. Students can't utilize the assessment tool if they don't understand the language within it.

Teacher Tip

The criteria/description per trait will be based on what students learned during the trait-introduction mini-lessons.

Teacher Tip

Encourage the use of definitives in rubrics. *All* and *few/none* clearly define the top and bottom levels of the rubric. This is a better option than identifying precise quantities.

Teacher Tip

Secondary teachers will build a rubric with *each class period* and then "merge" the criteria into a single document. This fosters student ownership but honors that the classroom teacher needs a common rubric for all classes.

Teacher Tip

 Incorporate the visual icons for each trait within the class writing rubric as it helps connect this tool to the 6-Trait introductory lessons.

Teacher Tip

Teacher-created rubrics often include phrases like "ideas are developed" or "ideas are arranged in a logical progression" or "sentences are well constructed." This is not kid-friendly lingo. After making the rubric *with* students, they can use it to self-assess and/or peer-assess.

Consider an alternative rubric-building approach

It's common to build a basic 6-Traits writing rubric with students during a single writer's workshop. However, sometimes students struggle to recall what each trait meant when it was introduced several days earlier (Section 6, pp. 43-50). A solution to that would be to build the rubric when conducting the trait introduction. Rather than building the rubric *after* introducing *all* the traits, build it *while* introducing *each* trait.

If each trait is introduced across two days/two mini-lessons, then the second mini-lesson could include building *just the single row* of the writing rubric. Rather than building the rubric vertically, it's built horizontally.

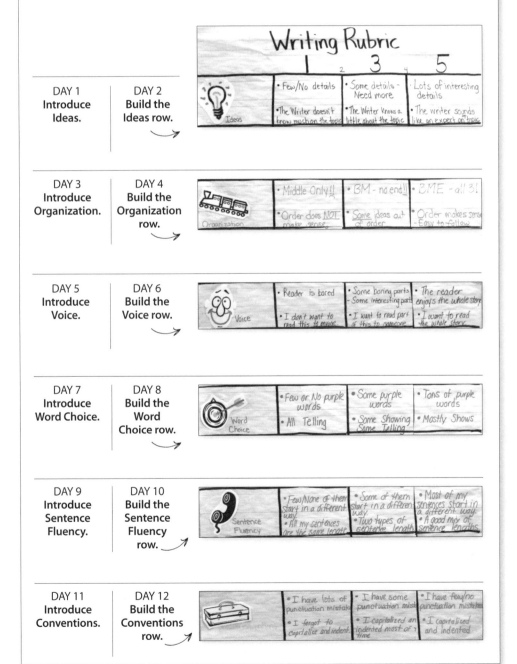

DAY 1 Introduce Ideas.	**DAY 2** Build the Ideas row.
DAY 3 Introduce Organization.	**DAY 4** Build the Organization row.
DAY 5 Introduce Voice.	**DAY 6** Build the Voice row.
DAY 7 Introduce Word Choice.	**DAY 8** Build the Word Choice row.
DAY 9 Introduce Sentence Fluency.	**DAY 10** Build the Sentence Fluency row.
DAY 11 Introduce Conventions.	**DAY 12** Build the Conventions row.

Teacher Tip

Rubrics can be created on large chart paper and/or typed within this editable Word document.

ONLINE RESOURCE

MINI-LESSON #3: Update the rubric frequently

As new skills are taught, expectations should increase. Consequently, as the year progresses, "up the ante" on the writing rubric.

Initially, the rubric criteria is general. It's based only on a basic trait introduction. However, as mini-lessons are taught, those skills have to be added to the rubric. This holds students accountable. Teach more, then expect more.

Such a mini-lesson might start like this: *Today we will take a few minutes to update our rubric. There are skills we have learned* (point to the yearlong 6-Traits bulletin board, p. 50), *that are not yet represented on our rubric.*

- Identify one new skill and the trait it falls under. *We learned that writers should select small, narrow, and manageable topics. That will help the trait of ideas.*
- *Let's add that to the rubric. How should we word it?*
- Then walk that skill down, adding criteria to levels 3 and 1.
- Identify another skill recently taught in a mini-lesson but not represented on the rubric. Identify the trait it targets and prepare to add it to the rubric.
- Continue this process until all recently learned skills have been added to the writing rubric.

If the rubric is written on chart paper, then literally cut apart the rubric and insert criteria, keeping all trait-specific skills together.

Within the online resource, it will be evident that the same marker color was used when the new skills were added to the growing rubric. This helps students see the related criteria per trait.

Independent Writing:
Continue within the current writing unit.

Launching the Writer's Workshop: Grades 3-12, Kristina Smekens and Maureen Scane
© 2017 Smekens Education Solutions, Inc.

Utilize one rubric for all writing units

It's not necessary to generate a separate rubric per writing unit/mode. If the traits embody the characteristics of *all good writing*, then it stands to reason that the same general criteria would be applicable to a persuasive essay, an informative report, and a narrative story.

Although the rubric language is specific enough to distinguish between levels, it's broad enough to be applicable to different modes. For example:

Ideas are well developed can be interpreted as:
- The plot is well developed in a narrative.
- The main ideas are well developed in an informative.
- The claims/reasons are well developed in a persuasive/argumentative.

Ideas are organized logically can be interpreted as:
- The plot moves in a chronological order in a narrative.
- Similar facts and quotes are grouped together in an informative.
- Reasons are organized to maximize the impact on the reader in a persuasive/argumentative.

Quotations add interest can be interpreted as:
- The character dialogue is interesting in a narrative.
- Expert quotes are interesting in an informative.
- Testimonials are powerful in a persuasive/argumentative.

Although most criteria is applicable across all writing, there are a few mode-specific skills. For example, a research paper might include:
- *Ideas— Information is used from three or more sources.*
- *Conventions— Citations are punctuated correctly.*

However, if after this research writing, the next assignment was to generate a narrative, these criteria are not applicable. To resolve this, don't generate a whole new rubric. Rather, delete the handful of irrelevant criteria on the typed rubric and *save as* "narrative rubric."

When this unit is over, resume using the complete rubric, continuing to grow it as new skills are learned (Mini-Lesson #3, p. 56).

MS & HS Teachers: Utilize one rubric for multiple grade levels

Although teachers are creating initial writing rubrics in every class, those working with multiple grade levels will merge the drafts together to produce a single assessment version (Teacher Tip, p. 54).

Rubric criteria can fit various writing units/modes *and* multiple grade levels. There are not many ways to say *The ideas are developed with many sentences* or *Includes lots of powerful action verbs.*

The key is interpreting what "many sentences" and "lots" means for sixth graders versus eighth graders or freshman versus AP seniors. (NOTE: This is true of most state assessment writing rubrics, as well. The same rubric is used for multiple grades levels but interpreted differently.)

Teacher Tip

If the rubric is posted in the classroom, tape paper overtop the irrelevant criteria covering it up for a particular assignment. When that unit is over, resume using the complete rubric by removing the covering.

Teacher Tip

Define rubric interpretations with anchor papers. Hang grade-appropriate writing samples with the corresponding rubric levels. This will depict what high, middle, and low writing looks like in grade 8 versus grade 6.

Assess the relevant traits

Just because there are six traits doesn't mean all six are scored within each writing assignment. *That would require a lot of assessing!* For most assignments, identify the 2-3 traits most relevant.

- Which traits did the mini-lesson instruction target?
- Which traits are most appropriate for this type/mode of writing?
- Which traits are appropriate to the amount of time students spent writing? Is it a first draft or a final draft?

Scoring for all 6 Traits is appropriate when the piece is a final draft. But for most other instances, consider paring down the traits assessed.

Be sure to communicate *which* traits are being scored per assignment. It's only fair for students to know the focus areas before they write. They shouldn't be guessing what the teacher wants.

Provide feedback to students

Since the rubric criteria is created with the students, expect them to use the tool in self-assessment. Each student could attach a copy of the rubric to his writing and mark what level per trait his writing earns.

Then the teacher scores using the same attached rubric. Provide specific feedback by highlighting rubric criteria that describes the piece. This is especially helpful when a writing scores a Level 2. Students see the weaknesses that plagued the writing based on criteria highlighted from Level 1 and what the strengths were according to highlighted criteria from Level 3.

Additional comments and feedback can be noted within the margins of the rubric. Indicate paragraph numbers that lack development, specific words that are weak, grammar skills needing attention, etc. Write comments on the rubric, rather than on the student's paper.

Convert rubric scores to grades

Video Clip Learn the do's and don'ts of getting a grade from a writing rubric. Watch "Convert Rubric Scores to Grades" via the online resource. This video article includes the hyperlink to the Rubric Calculator.

Teacher Tip

When scoring only 2-3 traits during a writing rubric, remove the rubric rows and *save as* "First Draft Compare-Contrast" or another assignment-specific rubric. Provide students a copy of this abbreviated rubric *before* they begin the assignment.

Teacher Tip

Although most students want the teacher to mark every convention error or propose revised sentence structures, they aren't learning anything. Teachers are not copy editors. Do not tell students what to correct. Rather, use the rubric to note weaknesses, provide additional instruction, and then leave it to the students to improve.

ONLINE RESOURCES

Teaching Ideas

SECTION 8

Writers communicate to the reader through the trait of ideas. They provide information, details, evidence, and explanation about a topic. It all starts with the trait of ideas.

However, for many students, this trait is often the weakest. General thoughts are mentioned but not elaborated. Reasons are stated but not developed. Evidence is listed but not explained. Students expect their readers to know what they mean rather than fleshing out their ideas wholly and completely.

To develop their ideas, students need explicit instruction on *how* to elaborate. They need to understand that when the teacher requests more details, this does not mean adding more undeveloped topic sentences. Rather, the goal is to add examples, evidence, and explanation to the ideas already stated.

Trait-Based Mini-Lessons

Mini-lessons for
PERSUASIVE, ARGUMENTATIVE, & INFORMATIVE WRITING UNITS

#1	p. 60	Narrow down writing topics
#2	p. 61	Generate a thesis statement
#3	p. 62	Align with the strongest position
#4	p. 63	Distinguish between details & development
#5	p. 64	Add "leg" sentences per "table-top" reason
#6	p. 65	Add information with definition details
#7	p. 66	Add interest with Snapple® details
#8	p. 67	Add specifics with name details
#9	p. 68	Add value with number details
#10	p. 69	Add description with comparison details
#11	p. 70	Add life with anecdotes
#12	p. 71	Add credibility with expert voices
#13	p. 72	Paraphrase author ideas
#14	p. 73	Incorporate citations
#15	p. 74	Stay on topic with a temporary title

Mini-lessons for
NARRATIVE WRITING UNITS

#1	p. 60	Narrow down writing topics
#4	p. 63	Distinguish between details & development
#6	p. 65	Add information with definition details
#8	p. 67	Add specifics with name details
#9	p. 68	Add value with number details
#10	p. 69	Add description with comparison details
#15	p. 74	Stay on topic with a temporary title

MINI-LESSON #1: Narrow down writing topics

Students often write about general subjects (e.g., turtles, Halloween, school, assisted suicide, the Holocaust, etc.). However, each of these topics is too broad. They require the writer to cover a lot of ground. Consequently, they skim the surface of the topic, mentioning a lot of facets but developing very little. This generates a "listy" piece. Read "Halloween."

Ask students to identify all the facets mentioned in the draft (e.g., costumes, trick-or-treating, candy, clown, etc.). Explain that with all of those subtopics, Halloween is too big. (Write "Halloween" in the large box on *Find the Smallest Topic* graphic organizer.)

 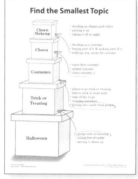 

- Select one idea mentioned in "Halloween" (e.g., trick-or-treating) and note it in the next box of the graphic organizer. However, just because it's smaller than Halloween doesn't mean it's small enough.
- Test it out. Identify smaller facets that would fall under this topic (e.g., costumes, candy, the neighborhood, the weather, etc.). Declare that trick-or-treating is still too broad.
- Select one facet of it— costumes— and write it in the next box.
- However, that topic would likely produce a list of costumes worn every year. Narrow to a single costume (e.g. clown). Write that in the next box. That is a small and narrow topic, but consider if it can be narrowed any more— without getting too small.
- One option would be to focus on a significant facet of the costume (e.g., clown makeup). Write that in the smallest box and read aloud "My Clown Face."
- Compare the small and interesting details in the second draft to the generic list of undeveloped ideas in the first piece.

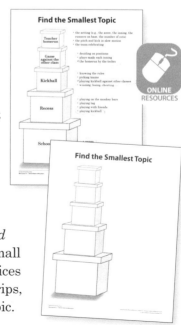

Narrow down a second broad subject (e.g., school) to identify a manageable topic.

Independent Writing:

Provide students with another copy of the *Find the Smallest Topic* graphic organizer. Pairs/Small groups select a broad subject from a list of choices (e.g., family, vacation, holidays, chores, field trips, etc.). Together they practice narrowing the topic.

Visual Triggers

Demonstrate the concept of shrinking a topic with nesting boxes or gift bags that diminish in size. Before the lesson, fold a copy of "My Clown Face" inside the smallest box or gift bag to read when it's time to reveal the final draft.

Follow-Up Lesson

This mini-lesson utilizes an informational topic. Show students how to also narrow topics when writing personal narratives. When the problem is revealed and resolved within five minutes, you know the topic is narrow.

Brainstorm moments in life that make for great five-minute stories (e.g., the final pitch of a ball game, a significant phone call, entering a surprise party, having a fight with a best friend, etc.).

Launching the Writer's Workshop: Grades 3-12, Kristina Smekens and Maureen Scane
© 2017 Smekens Education Solutions, Inc.

MINI-LESSON #2: Generate a thesis statement

Strong writing includes an overriding thesis statement that captures the topic and purpose of the writing. If the thesis is too broad (e.g., *There have been a lot of technological changes.*), the reader assumes the writer will tackle all of the facets of that topic.

Reveal the broadest thesis statement at the bottom of *Narrow Down the Thesis* handout. Demonstrate its weakness with a series of assumptions.

- *I expect this writer plans to address ALL types of technology, including advances in medicine, automobiles, cell phones, computers, prosthetics, travel, etc.*
- *Since there is no specific time frame included, I expect this writer will cover technological changes from ALL of history.*
- *I expect this writer will provide ALL the positive and negative impacts of ALL technology for ALL people.*

The thesis provides a clear plan of what the writer will address. But what many students don't realize is that this same sentence also identifies what the writer will *not* address.

After pointing out these problems with such a vague and broad thesis, reveal the next "smaller" thesis statement on the handout. Continue to question the narrowness while showing the subsequent topic sentences on the *Narrow Down the Thesis* handout.

When the final thesis statement is revealed, note that:
- The broad subject matter (e.g., *technological changes*) is still written into the statement. However, it includes the specific facets that will be addressed, implying what the writer will *not* cover.
- A narrow thesis tends to be long. In order to put parameters on the topic, it requires additional words and phrases. A short thesis sentence often indicates a broad subject.
- It avoids words that imply all-inclusive language or absolutes (e.g., *always, never, every time, all, none,* etc.), as these are typically impossible to prove.
- It doesn't ask something; it declares something. Thesis statements are never questions.
- In persuasive and argumentative writing, the topic is debatable. Therefore, the thesis takes a stand or conveys an opinion.

Independent Writing:
Students attempt to write a thesis statement and then share it with a partner. Peers provide feedback based on what they assume will be addressed within that topic. Using that, the writer revises his thesis adding details that identify the narrow focus.

Teacher Tip
Execute this lesson *after* teaching students how to identify a narrow topic to write about (Mini-Lesson #1, p. 60).

Visual Triggers
Shrinking nesting boxes or gift bags (Mini-Lesson #1, p. 60) are again appropriate triggers for this lesson. They mimic the narrow scope of a thesis statement.

Follow-Up Lessons
Introductory paragraphs include more than a topic sentence or thesis statement. For more information, see:
- Persuasive/Argumentative Introductions, Mini-Lesson #13, p. 90.
- Informative Introductions, Mini-Lesson #15, p. 92.
- Narrative Introductions, Mini-Lesson #17, p. 94.

Teacher Tip
This mini-lesson is a great addition to any type of research unit. Execute it after students have collected information on their topics and are ready to formulate the focus of their writings.

Mentor Text

...for Multiple Perspectives

Arnie, the Doughnut, L. Keller
Click, Clack, Moo, Cows That Type,
  D. Cronin
The Day the Crayons Quit, D. Daywalt
Hey, Little Ant, P. Hoose
Spoon, A. Krouse Rosenthal
Voices in the Park, A. Browne

Video Clips

Build a *Two-Perspectives T-Chart* using debatable information found on *www.procon.org*. Or use content learned from two infomercials on the same product (e.g., ShamWow®).

Follow-Up Lessons

Eventually, tweak the *Two Perspectives T-Chart* to include a middle column for text titles. For additional instruction on providing citations, see Mini-Lesson #14, p. 73.

There are often more than two perspectives to an issue. See the Follow-Up Lesson on p. 81 for how to juggle three or more perspectives.

MINI-LESSON #3: Align with the strongest position

When writing a persuasive or argumentative piece, the writer should *not* hastily choose a position based on personal opinion. This type of writing requires information, proof, evidence, examples, support, etc.

Reveal the *Two-Perspectives T-Chart*. Explain that each column represents a different viewpoint on a debatable issue. For example:

- Eat Arnie versus don't eat Arnie (based on *Arnie, the Doughnut*).
- Squish the ant versus don't squish the ant (based on *Hey, Little Ant*).
- Spoon has a great life versus boring life (based on *Spoon*).
- Scientists should test versus should not test on animals.
- Consumers should purchase versus should not purchase a ShamWow.
- Polar Pops (a brand of fountain drink) are great versus pitiful.

Teach students that proof— not preference— should determine which side they align with. In order to do that, model this four-step process.

1. Identify the two perspectives at the top of the *T-Chart*.
2. List reasons and evidence that support both viewpoints.
3. Reread the lists considering which position is strongest. *Which has the most evidence? Which has the most powerful proof?*
4. Align with the perspective that presents the strongest argument.

Many students jump right to Step 4— skipping steps 1-3. If the student chooses a side *before* conducting any research, then he may craft a thesis statement he cannot support.

Clarify that a written argument is *not* a reflection of a student's personal beliefs or morals. Students do not have to personally agree with the side they are arguing. It's based solely on the reading and research collected. (This is reinforced with the use of third-person pronouns *they, some, experts,* and *proponents,* rather than the first-person *I*.) Compare this approach to defense attorneys who don't agree with their clients and yet fight to prove their innocence. They simply have to put together the strongest case possible.

Independent Writing:

Provide 1-2 informational texts on a single debatable issue. Students execute the four steps in groups to determine the strongest perspective. NOTE: Students are *not* producing an entire essay. They are simply recording information per viewpoint on the *Two-Perspectives T-Chart*. Plan for students to repeat the process more than once.

NOTE: Save the *Two-Perspectives T-Charts* students create. They will be useful in future persuasive/argumentative mini-lessons (Mini-Lessons #8 - #10, pp. 85-87).

Launching the Writer's Workshop: Grades 3-12, Kristina Smekens and Maureen Scane
© 2017 Smekens Education Solutions, Inc.

MINI-LESSON #4: Distinguish between details & development

"Developed" writing includes ideas that are elaborated. That's the secret! Every idea or reason stated must be followed by a second, third, and/or fourth sentence that provides support. The opposite of "developed" is "listy" writing—when students just provide the idea or reason with no follow-up sentences.

To combat this, clarify that details are different than development. Details are just words. They are often adjectives or phrases added to an existing sentence. Whereas when ideas are truly developed, they include multiple sentences that provide explanation, examples, description, evidence, proof. Demonstrate development with a concrete object.

Video Clip

For more information about this lesson concept, watch "Clarify 'developed' versus 'details'" via the online resource.

Visual Triggers

A light bulb gets brighter and brighter with more information.

A balloon expands with each additional breath of informa-tion.

An image goes from black and white to full color with more information.

A "table-top" reason is held up by additional "leg" sentences.

ONLINE RESOURCES

ORIGINAL

A Weekend Walk

This weekend I took my dog for a long walk. We went far and saw a lot. It was fun.

REVISED

A Weekend Walk

This weekend, August 10, 2007, I took my four-year-old Golden Retriever Mazie for a long walk. We strolled down Main Street and Wayne Street looking for something to do. We waved to Mrs. Lucy and Mr. Roberts at the pharmacy. We heard the laughter of people mingling in the McDonald's parking lot, and we visited with a round woman walking her black-and-white speckled Dalmatian.

We continued our adventure; we went down to Tower Park in Warren, IN. It's about six blocks from our house. The flowers that lined the walkway were ... Mazie walked quickly by them with her ... to the blooms. I think she was getting a ... sweet fragrance.

... walked the curve of the sidewalk. Mazie ... de and began pouncing excitedly. We went ... n the slide together seven times. With ... I had to haul my 20-pound dog up the ... e top of the slide. It was like carrying a ... of sand— awkward and heavy. But it was ... effort. Sliding down the sleek aluminum strip was hilarious.

Starting out about 4:30p.m., we were gone for almost two hours. It was a great way to spend the afternoon.

ONLINE RESOURCES

Provide an undeveloped example (e.g., original "A Weekend Walk"). Point out how skimpy and/or "listy" it is. Then reveal its revised version. Discuss the impact of the additional information.

Reveal a second "listy" writing sample. Model how to develop the ideas by generating additional sentences orally. Make frequent connections to the visual trigger introduced (e.g., *All these sentences are making the topic brighter, fuller, more color-ful, or more supported.*).

Conclude the lesson distinguishing between de-velopment and length. Although the revision is longer, the real secret is that each idea is fuller. Anyone can make their writing longer by adding more single-sentence ideas. Those pieces are still "listy." However, adding sentences to support each original idea makes the ideas fuller and more developed.

Independent Writing:

Students return to their writers' notebooks and identify a "listy" piece. Have them write additional sentences to support the original ideas stated in the first draft. (See Mini-Lesson #2, p. 33 for ways to make room for revision.)

Follow-Up Lessons

Don't plan to take this draft through the entire revision pro-cess. This is just a quick attempt at developing ideas. Follow this initial lesson with explicit instruc-tion on various types of sentences students could add (Mini-Lessons #6 - #13, pp. 65-72).

Visual Triggers

Any table can serve as a trigger for this mini-lesson. It's just more fun to bring in a real-world artifact like the pizza-box table.

Follow-Up Lesson

Lay the groundwork for paragraph indents. Casually mention that each table becomes its own paragraph (Mini-Lesson #3, p. 124).

Follow-Up Lesson

This mini-lesson demonstrates idea development during the revision process. However, eventually, it should be incorporated into the pre-writing stage. Teach students how to note their big ideas/reasons and jot the key details about each on the *Table-Top Sentences & Supporting-Leg Details* graphic organizer. Each table is then fleshed out into a paragraph when composing the first draft. See the "Indian Village" example below.

MINI-LESSON #5: Add "leg" sentences per "table-top" reason

Students are pretty good at listing ideas or reasons, but they often leave each one underdeveloped and/or under-supported. They assume the reader will fill in the blanks of their thinking.

Start this lesson explaining the function of the small plastic "table" within a pizza delivery box. The legs are the key; they hold up the lid so it doesn't squish the pizza toppings.

Compare this to the students' writing. Reveal an undeveloped or "listy" writing sample (e.g., "Spring Break"). Identify each idea as a table top sitting on the floor because there aren't additional "leg" sentences to hold it up. Using the *Table-Top Sentences & Supporting-Leg Details* graphic organizer, transfer each main idea/reason to a table top.

Model how to add information to the table-top sentence *Florida is a great place to go in the winter.*

- Rotate the handout to show it requires some "leg" sentences to hold it up.
- Think Aloud asking *Why is Florida a great place? What could I say about it to prove it's a great place?*
- Jot 3-4 specifics on the legs below the table top.

Remind students that tables don't stand on one leg, and they're unsteady with only two legs. But like the pizza-box table, they are sturdy and solid with three or more "leg" sentences. Consequently, add three or more supporting sentences in the sample about visiting Florida.

Model the next undeveloped table-top sentence (e.g., *Roughing it outdoors while camping is an option.*) Then support students generating additional "leg" sentences for the remaining two table tops.

Independent Writing:

Provide students with a "listy" writing sample and a corresponding *Table-Top Sentences & Supporting-Leg Details* graphic organizer. Additional examples include:

- Taking care of a pet.
- Supporting a sports team.
- Attending a school dance.

Working with a partner, students develop each main idea with 3-4 additional "leg" sentences of support.

Launching the Writer's Workshop: Grades 3-12, Kristina Smekens and Maureen Scane
© 2017 Smekens Education Solutions, Inc.

MINI-LESSON #6: Add information with definition details

Start this mini-lesson with a connection to reading. Review how authors provide nearby clues as to what unfamiliar words mean in order to support reader comprehension. Today's mini-lesson will reveal how students can include context clues to aid their readers, too.

Although writers attempt to use precise word choice, the reader may not know what the terms mean. Thus, students need to occasionally explain the meaning of key words within their writing. Without definition details, readers feel left out and/or confused about the information.

- Reveal examples from the *Definition Details* handout and/or those collected from recently read text. (Reveal examples from literature and informational text.)
- Note how each sentence provides the reader a little additional background information.
- Compare these author techniques to those listed on the *8 Types of Definition Details* handout.
- Notice the use of key phrases to introduce the definition or explanation (e.g., *that means, this means, which means,* etc.) and how it impacts the sentence structure.

Model how to write a definition detail.
- Read aloud an anchor paper.
- Identify a word that readers may not understand.
- Select one of the eight ways to insert a definition detail.
- Integrate this information within the same or following sentence.
- Model a different technique to incorporate a definition detail for the *same* word. This demonstrates there is more than one way to structure a definition detail.
- Allow students to offer additional suggestions using other options listed on the *8 Types of Definition Details* handout.

Independent Writing:

Students return to previous writings to identify 3-5 precise words that could include a definition detail. (They do not have to all come from the same piece.) Have them insert a definition detail for each word within the original sentence or the following one.

Teacher Tip

Definition details are one type of supporting "leg" sentence to add to a "table-top" idea (Mini-Lesson #5, p. 64).

Teacher Tip

Writers who incorporate definition details demonstrate that they have a strong sense of audience awareness. This, in turn, impacts the trait of voice.

Mentor Text

Rick Bragg's *New York Times* article "Skeleton Plunges Face First Back into the Winter Games" includes a definition detail within paragraph 23.

Follow-Up Lessons

Reveal various punctuation marks that set off a definition detail.

Once students know how to add a definition detail, push them to occasionally include an extended definition. These include the explanation of the word's meaning *and* a comparison via a simile, metaphor, analogy, anecdote, etc.

Teacher Tip

Snapple® details are one type of supporting "leg" sentence to add to a "table-top" idea (Mini-Lesson #5, p. 64).

Teacher Tip

Writers who incorporate Snapple details demonstrate they have a strong sense of audience awareness by attempting to engage their readers with intriguing information. This, in turn, impacts the trait of voice.

Mentor Text

Rick Bragg's *New York Times* article "Skeleton Plunges Face First Back into the Winter Games" includes a Snapple detail at the beginning of paragraph 11.

Teacher Tip

This mini-lesson is a great addition to any research unit.

MINI-LESSON #7: Add interest with Snapple® details

Dispel the myth that informative or research writing is the "boring" writing. It's only boring if writers make it boring.

When generating informative, persuasive, and/or argumentative writings, students need to collect and include more than just the *important* information. They also must look for the *interesting*. If the writing is intended to teach the reader, then it should reveal something the reader didn't know about the topic.

Reveal lids from Snapple beverages or examples from *www.snapple.com/real-facts*. Read aloud a couple of "Snapple Real Facts," noting the various reactions of the students (e.g., *No way! Seriously!? Wow! You're kidding! Really?!*). Define Snapple Facts in writing as facts that go beyond the "no duh" details and surprise the reader with something.

Pass out Snapple lids (or copy "Real Facts" from the website). Ask students to read and share 1-2 of the most surprising "Snapple Real Facts." Explain that writers should incorporate such high-interest facts within their informative, persuasive, and argumentative writing.

Reveal excerpts from informational text that include Snapple facts. Ask students to listen for an interesting, surprising, or intriguing detail. Then reread the text *without* those details/sentences. Discuss the impact of Snapple facts in nonfiction writing.

Independent Writing:

Provide a *Snapple® Facts* handout to each student. While reading/researching their topics, they are to be on the lookout for relevant Snapple facts. Students will record them in the circle "lids" of the handout. Be sure they include the source of the information, too.

MINI-LESSON #8: Add specifics with name details

Start this mini-lesson with a quick activity. Using scratch paper, have students draw the following— a dog, a sandwich, and a vehicle. Have students compare their quick sketches with a peer. Note how differently they all interpreted those generic nouns. Now, have them draw a specific version of each— a poodle, a cheeseburger, and a monster truck. Note how the specific names created a much clearer picture in each of their minds. This is what writers attempt to do; they want to communicate clearly and precisely to their readers.

Teacher Tip

Brand-name details are one type of supporting "leg" sentence to add to a "table-top" idea (Mini-Lesson #5, p. 64).

Now reveal a generic or no-brand product (e.g., toaster pastries, facial tissues, etc.). Then show a brand-name version of the same product (e.g., Pop Tarts®, Puffs®, etc.). Ask students which version they prefer their parents to buy and why.

Their responses might include:
- *The name brand one tastes better, works better, etc. You aren't always sure what to expect with the generic version.*
- *The name-brand one usually comes in packaging that is more colorful and more interesting.*
- *It costs more, yes, but it's worth it.*

Reveal "generic" and "brand-name" versions of the same topic.

Teacher Tip

It's easier to appreciate the power of specific details if the strong and weak examples are on parallel topics. Consequently, before executing the mini-lesson, identify a couple of strong "brand-name" excerpts and revise them to create "generic" versions, too.

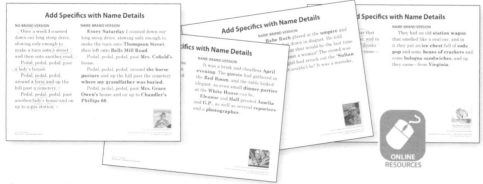

Compare the two versions.
- When a writer uses a specific name detail, the reader knows exactly what to visualize. The picture is very clear.
- Specific names add life and interest to the piece.
- "Brand-name" nouns don't actually have to be proper nouns. They may just identify a specific type of something, provide a specific description, or refer to a single item.
- It's more work to think of specific details, but it's worth it.

Mentor Text

Rick Bragg's *New York Times* article "Skeleton Plunges Face First Back into the Winter Games" provides many specific names and nouns within paragraphs 14 and 18.

Independent Writing:

Students return to a previous draft and replace 10 generic nouns with specific name details using the strikethrough revision strategy and a colored pen (Mini-Lesson #2, p. 33).

MINI-LESSON #9: Add value with number details

Study the various mentor text excerpts in the right column of the *Add Value with Number Details* handout. Compare the original sentence to the revised version where the specifics have been removed. *How do the numbers add to the reader's comprehension? Does the information have the same impact when the specific quantities are removed?*

There is nothing vague or abstract about an idea when numbers are presented. Writers use numbers to communicate clearly to the reader. Numbers are precise and exact.

Number details have a place in all modes of writing.
- In persuasive and informative writing, numbers add importance, significance, and credibility.
- In narrative writing, numbers make the story seem more believable. There is a truthfulness to number details.

Model how to add precise number details to an anchor paper.
- Read the piece, looking for places where a specific number would help the reader better understand or comprehend the topic. *Where is the information a little general? Where is it abstract and hard to truly understand the point? Where would numbers add power and importance?*
- Think Aloud, *What kind of number detail would be appropriate to fill in some of those holes?* Study the various quantitative details within the *Add Value with Number Details* handout.
- Be choosey on where to add in number details; too many numbers isn't good either.
- Use the blanks in the handout to add more number types.

Independent Writing:

Return to a previous writing (or start a new piece) intentionally weaving in number details to add more specificity and reality to the topic.

ADD VALUE WITH **NUMBER DETAILS**

date	October 12, 2005
age	4 years old
quantity	16 chairs
temperature	87 degrees
time	7:30 a.m.
elapsed time	90 minutes
speed	70 mph
weight	65 pounds
length, height	18 inches
percentage	90%
code (model #, ID #, part #)	item #4757
how many times/ frequency	3 times
price	$29
score	53-51

MINI-LESSON #10: Add description with comparison details

When a reader lacks background knowledge on a topic, he may struggle to comprehend. Consequently, when writing on a less familiar topic, students need to incorporate comparison details. This is where the writer connects a new or unfamiliar idea to something that the reader already knows about.

Share various mentor text examples from the *Convey Meaning Through Comparisons* handout.

- Identify the comparisons being made.
- Hypothesize that the author anticipated reader confusion and therefore added in the extra detail.
- Note the universal items being referenced within each comparison. These are well-known things.
- Reread the statements *without* the comparisons. Discuss the possible effect on the reader's comprehension. Comparisons make it possible for a reader to fully understand complex information, even if he may lack background knowledge.

Return to the *Convey Meaning Through Comparisons* handout. Discuss the different ways authors convey meaning through comparisons. For example:
1. The reader gains insight or knowledge on a topic they know little about when it's compared to something they know a lot about.
2. The reader empathizes with something they have never experienced when it's compared to something they have experienced.
3. The reader more clearly visualizes something they have never seen personally when it's compared to something they have seen.
4. The reader can better appreciate the magnitude or significance of something that may have initially been abstract or vague.

Model how to incorporate a comparison detail.
- Reveal an anchor paper or excerpt of text on a less familiar topic— one that most students would *not* know about.
- Identify a place where it's important the reader understand the point, and therefore it would benefit from a comparison detail.
- Think Aloud about the information itself and then brainstorm everyday objects or situations that are similar. The key is to identify something everyone can relate to.
- Select the object or situation that fits best and then craft a phrase or sentence utilizing a connecting word (e.g., *like, just like, as, reminds me of*, etc.) to show the comparison.
- Insert the comparison detail into the text.
- Reread the revised portion and ask the students if the point seems more clear with the comparison detail added.

Independent Writing:

Students find places in previous drafts where the reader may lack background knowledge. (NOTE: If students can't find such a place, have them swap papers. Peers can more easily point out terms or concepts that are unclear.) Students revise the identified sentences to include comparison details.

Teacher Tip

Comparison details are one type of supporting "leg" sentence to add to a "table-top" idea (Mini-Lesson #5, p. 64).

Mentor Text

Rick Bragg's *New York Times* article "Skeleton Plunges Face First Back into the Winter Games" includes memorable comparison details within paragraphs 1, 16, and 32.

ONLINE RESOURCE

Teacher Tip

Connect this lesson to specific types of figurative language that compare two ideas (e.g., similes, metaphors, analogies, allusions, etc.).

Teacher Tip

Clarify that this technique does not include stringing adjectives together. It's not description with adjectives. It's information with comparisons. It equates an unfamiliar item, idea, or concept with a familiar one.

Follow-Up Lesson

Clarify helpful comparisons versus overused clichés. For more information, read the article "Teach Students How to Omit Clichés" via the online resource.

ONLINE RESOURCE

MINI-LESSON #11: Add life with anecdotes

Facts, statistics, and expert quotes comprise much of an informative or persuasive/argumentative piece. Readers wade through sentence after sentence of heavy information, unfamiliar vocabulary, and abstract statistics. An occasional anecdote can prove a point in a softer way. Anecdotes add real-world relevance to the information; they humanize the information.

An anecdote is a mini-story. It's a relevant scenario, situation, or depiction that further drives home the writer's point. The combination of quantitative facts with softer qualitative anecdotes makes for a nice mixture of support.

Reveal mentor text that includes a heavy dose of statistics and facts followed by a narrative anecdote. Emphasize the following:

- The narrative paragraph provides the reader a much needed break from the intense information overload.
- These mini-stories are a writer's opportunity to entertain, amuse, inform, or even shock the reader. They add voice to the writing.
- They give the reader insight into how those involved felt during that time. Anecdotes are engaging and compelling.
- An anecdote offers proof or support. It strengthens the writer's point. It's a situation or incident that illustrates a key point.
- The secret to a well-written anecdote is to strip it of any unnecessary information. Use the story to make the point efficiently and succinctly.
- Notice how authors introduce an anecdote (e.g., *This was the case for... For instance... This point is illustrated by...*).
- The mini-story can describe a real person or situation or a hypothetical one.

REAL EXAMPLES	HYPOTHETICAL EXAMPLES
• Retell someone's actual story. • Describe an incident that has happened previously. • Provide a testimonial from a real person directly involved or affected.	• Describe a possible scene, scenario, or situation. • Depict a common occurrence. • Create a plausible story about an imaginary person.

Independent Writing:

Students return to a previous informative, persuasive, or argumentative writing to identify a place where the data and evidence are abundant. Insert an anecdote— real or hypothetical— to further illustrate the point and humanize the information.

Teacher Tip

Anecdotes are one type of supporting "leg" sentence to add to a "table-top" idea (Mini-Lesson #5, p. 64).

Mentor Text

Rick Bragg's *New York Times* article "Skeleton Plunges Face First Back into the Winter Games" includes an emotional anecdote in paragraph 21 that adds life to the facts and stats listed in the previous paragraph.

Launching the Writer's Workshop: Grades 3-12, Kristina Smekens and Maureen Scane
© 2017 Smekens Education Solutions, Inc.

MINI-LESSON #12: Add credibility with expert voices

A writer's point is communicated more powerfully when an expert supports it. Quotations from authorities add credibility to the writer's information and position. They prove that the writer's ideas, reasons, and position are valid and worthy of consideration.

However, it's more than just finding a quote and kerplunking it into the piece. The real power in a quote is identifying which expert voices to include. Students should be choosey in selecting which experts get space in their writing. Remind them that this is *their* writing, and therefore it should be full of *their* ideas, not someone else's. Consequently, direct quotes should be used sparingly.

Teach students to discern when a direct quote is worthy— see the *Quote Authorities* handout.

Clarify that the sentiment of the expert's words may be strong but not worthy of direct quote. In these instances, students should utilize an indirect quotation. This is when the writer paraphrases or rewords the quote and credits the source. This is addressed in a separate lesson (Mini-Lesson #13, p. 72).

Reveal an informative, persuasive, or argumentative writing sample that includes too many direct quotes. Read and Think Aloud about which statements are worthy of quoting using the *Quote Authorities* handout.

With only the strongest quotes remaining in the writing sample, explain that an expert quote isn't valuable if the reader doesn't understand its relevance. Consequently, the writer must follow each direct quotation with a sentence or two of explanation.

- *What does the quote mean?*
- *Why is it important enough to include in this piece?*
- *What is the purpose of this information?*
- *How is it relevant to the topic?*
- *What does it matter?*
- *What does it prove?*
- *What is the impact of this quote?*

By adding this information, the writer is integrating the quote into the piece rather than just dumping it there.

Independent Writing:

Students reread previous pieces with direct quotes included. Working with a peer, have them read aloud a piece and identify if the direct quote is powerful enough to remain.

- If it is, adhere a sticky note to the quote and mark it with a star or asterisk. Then write the additional sentences of restatement and explanation.
- If it is not worthy, adhere a sticky note to the quote and mark it with an **X.**

Teacher Tip

Expert quotes are one type of supporting "leg" sentence to add to a "table-top" idea (Mini-Lesson #5, p. 64).

Mentor Text

There are excellent expert quotes throughout Rick Bragg's *New York Times* article "Skeleton Plunges Face First Back into the Winter Games." Two particularly strong examples are in paragraphs 4 and 40.

Follow-Up Lessons

This lesson focuses on *what* to quote. Subsequent lessons need to include *how* to incorporate the quoted words into the writing. This includes how to:

- Introduce the quote.
- Quote a complete sentence.
- Quote part of a sentence.
- Represent omitted words with an ellipsis.
- Confirm the words are copied exactly.
- Cite the source (Mini-Lesson #14, p. 73).

Follow-Up Lesson

Weaker quotes should be paraphrased (Mini-Lesson #13, p. 72).

Teacher Tip

Paraphrased ideas are one type of supporting "leg" sentence to add to a "table-top" idea (Mini-Lesson #5, p. 64).

Teacher Tip

Teach students both ways to include expert ideas into their writing and provide each student with a back-to-back copy of *Reasons to Paraphrase* (p. 72) and *Quote Authorities* (p. 71).

Video Clip

Connect the steps of paraphrasing to a bodily-kinesthetic hand signal.

Teacher Tip

Individual pages from nonfiction picture books are a great source to practice paraphrasing.

Follow-Up Lesson

Introduce the fifth step to paraphrasing: return to the original text to verify accuracy of names, numbers, spellings, and to gather source information for the citation (Mini-Lesson #14, p. 73).

MINI-LESSON #13: Paraphrase author ideas

There are two ways writers include expert ideas into their writing— direct quotes (Mini-Lesson #12, p. 71) and paraphrasing— restating someone else's opinion or idea into their own words.

There are several advantages to paraphrasing. For example, the writer maintains control of the voice, rather than giving it over to an expert. The writer can also package the idea using words and synonyms that heighten (or decrease) the impact of the message. Not to mention, paraphrasing often includes a shorter, more succinct version of the original.

Discuss the *Reasons to Paraphrase* handout. Then introduce the 4-step paraphrasing process.

1. **Read** a nonfiction excerpt (e.g.,*Walk with a Wolf*).
2. **Remove** the text by turning it over, minimizing the screen, turning away from it, or covering it up. The writer inherently begins to memorize or copy the original if he stares at it long enough.
3. **Explain** the opinion/idea. A writer cannot paraphrase an idea if he didn't first understand it. Comprehension is essential.
4. **Write/Type** the explanation. Without looking back at the original passage, the writer jots down what he just said in Step 3.

ORIGINAL EXCERPT	PARAPHRASED INFORMATION
If there is plenty of food around, all pack members will feed at once. But if meat is scarce, the strongest wolves will eat first— and the youngest, the cubs, last.	*When there is enough food, all wolves eat at the same time. However, if it's limited, then the strongest wolves take advantage and feed first.*

A paraphrase captures the sentiment of the original version but uses different vocabulary. Synonyms are how a writer ensures he has "put the idea into his own words." In the example, the author used *scarce* and *eat first*, but the paraphrase included *limited* and *take advantage*.

Reveal a second short excerpt. Guide students through the four steps. CAUTION: If a student cannot explain the passage aloud to a peer (Step 3), then he should repeat steps 1-3 before writing anything on paper. Remember, comprehension is key to paraphrasing.

Independent Writing:

Return to previous writings marked with an **X** from Mini-Lesson #12, p. 71. Remind students that they deemed these as *not* worthy of a direct quote. Consequently, they will paraphrase each one applying the 4-step process.

MINI-LESSON #14: Incorporate citations

Review previous lessons on quoting experts (Mini-Lesson #12, p. 71) and/
or paraphrasing their ideas (Mini-Lesson #13, p. 72). Those lessons targeted
what was said. This lesson focuses on *where* that information was originally
stated. This is referred to as citing or attributing the source.

Define plagiarism.
- Plagiarism is when the writer repeats someone else's words or ideas—
  quoted exactly or paraphrased— but does *not* attribute the original
  source.
- Even a paraphrase must include a citation. Unless the words or ideas are
  solely those of the writer (or they are considered general knowledge), they
  must be attributed to someone else.
- Plagiarism can happen accidentally or it can be intentional.

Reveal the *Incorporate Citations* handout.
- Explain that a citation includes two facets— 1) *which* text and 2) *where* in
  that text the original information can be found.
- When information is being pulled from
  multiple texts, the generic "According to
  the text..." phrase will no longer suffice.
  Expect students to identify the specific
  author and/or text title that each quote/
  paraphrase came from.
- Explain how to combine the *which* and
  where sourcing information to create the
  citation.

Model how to incorporate the citation.
- Return to the *5 Steps to Paraphrasing an
  Author's Idea* handout (p. 72).
- Reiterate the final step has the writer
  return to the original text to confirm accuracy *and* collect the citation information.
- Reveal direct quotes and/or paraphrases
  from previous pieces (Mini-Lessons #12
  and #13, pp. 71-72). Point out that the
  source is missing from each of these examples.
- Reread one quote/paraphrase, recall *which* text was the original source of
  the information, and retrieve it.
- Flip through that text. Identify *where* in the text the original information
  can be found (e.g., page number, paragraph number, line number, etc.).
- Craft a citation phrase that combines the *which* and *where* information.
- Add the citation into the same sentence as the quote/paraphrase.
- Demonstrate how the citation can be added before the quote/paraphrase
  or after it.

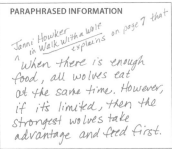

Independent Writing:
Return to the direct quotes and/or paraphrases generated during the writing
times that followed Mini-Lessons #12 and #13, pp. 71-72. Integrate the citation information for each.

Video Clip

For more information about this
lesson concept, watch "Weave the
What, Which, & Where into Textual
Citations" via the online resource.

Teacher Tip

Students must learn to maintain a
list of sources tied directly to their
quotes or paraphrases when they
are first conducting research.

Teacher Tip

This mini-lesson focuses on the
sourcing that happens *within*
the piece. However, it does not
replace the alphabetical list of
sources cited at the end of the
writing (i.e., *Works Cited*/MLA,
References/APA).

NOTE: A *Bibliography* is different
than *Works Cited* and *References*.
A Bibliography includes all of the
material the writer consulted,
whether or not it was cited within
the writing or not.

Teacher Tip

Before this lesson, identify a couple of short and grade-appropriate writing samples that are *mostly* on topic.

Teacher Tip

Initially conduct this lesson with anchor papers that include obvious off-topic sentences. But, as students get better at identifying "Fruit Loop" sentences, reveal examples that stray only a little off topic.

Teacher Tip

The thesis statement can serve as the main-idea title that all the other sentences should be about. If there is no temporary title, students can highlight the topic sentence or thesis statement to execute this strategy.

Follow-Up Lesson

This mini-lesson is applied in revision. However, writers must learn to stay on topic when composing the first draft. This is achieved with a temporary title. A label at the top of the piece is a constant reminder that each sentence written should be on point; it should match that title. After the draft is completed, the writer revises the temporary title for a more polished version (Mini-Lesson #19, p. 96).

MINI-LESSON #15: Stay on topic with a temporary title

Cereal-box titles alert the shopper to the type of breakfast food inside. The title of any writing does the same thing; it alerts readers to the information they should expect inside the piece. A consumer doesn't expect to find a Fruit Loop® inside a Cheerios® box. And a reader doesn't expect to find off-topic sentences that don't relate to the title. Every sentence should fit or match the title.

Reveal an anchor paper (e.g., "Destructive Puppy"). Explain that all of the sentences inside this piece should be about that topic (e.g., a puppy being destructive).

- Highlight the title.
- Read the first sentence aloud. Determine if the sentence is a Cheerio and on topic or a Fruit Loop and off topic. *Is this a detail about the puppy? Does this explain why the puppy is destructive? Does this sentence explain the destruction?*
- If it's on topic, then highlight it as it matches the title. If it's off topic, then strikethrough the sentence to indicate it should be cut from the draft.
- Repeat this process with the second sentence, and third, and so on.

Execute this with a second anchor paper, this time with the students' help. Again, reread the title after every sentence and check if they match. (NOTE: If the piece doesn't have a title already, then have the students reread and jot a simple 2-3 word label at the top that identifies what it's about.)

Independent Writing:

Students work with partners to reread a previous writing. Pairs will read each sentence together determining if it is on-topic (highlight it) or off-topic (strikethrough it). Once the pair has read one sample together, then they read the other student's writing.

Teaching Organization

SECTION 9

To achieve strong organization, writers need to purposefully plan the three parts of a piece. They must consider how to start the piece in an attention-grabbing way. They must determine how best to conclude the information in a memorable way. But the real secret to organization lies within the body.

The bulk of the writing is within the middle sentences and paragraphs. It's here where readers tend to get lost in a writer's helter-skelter sharing of information.

Mastering the trait of organization requires that related information is grouped and presented in a logical order. When the writer builds on individual ideas and transitions among key points, he achieves the ultimate goal— cohesion. This doesn't happen accidentally. Students require explicit instruction on how to create a unified piece that is easy to follow.

Trait-Based Mini-Lessons

Mini-lessons for
PERSUASIVE & ARGUMENTATIVE WRITING UNITS

P

#1	p. 76	List, group, & label related ideas
#2	p. 77	List & group details *before* writing
#6	p. 83	Answer *what* & *why* in constructed responses
#7	p. 84	Adapt Yes, MA'AM to fit longer essays
#8	p. 85	Reveal persuasive reasons intentionally
#9	p. 86	Convert a persuasive to an argument
#10	p. 87	Present both sides of an argument
#11	p. 88	Create transitions *within* paragraphs
#12	p. 89	Create transitions *among* paragraphs
#13	p. 90	Craft persuasive/argumentative introductions
#14	p. 91	Craft persuasive/argumentative conclusions
#19	p. 96	Generate titles that grab the reader

Mini-lessons for
INFORMATIVE WRITING UNITS

I

#1	p. 76	List, group, & label related ideas
#2	p. 77	List & group details *before* writing
#3	pp. 78-79	Organize information sequentially
#4	pp. 80-81	Organize compare-contrast information
#5	p. 82	Organize information categorically
#6	p. 83	Answer *what* & *why* in constructed responses
#7	p. 84	Adapt Yes, MA'AM to fit longer essays
#11	p. 88	Create transitions *within* paragraphs
#12	p. 89	Create transitions *among* paragraphs
#15	p. 92	Craft informative introductions
#16	p. 93	Craft informative conclusions
#19	p. 96	Generate titles that grab the reader

Mini-lessons for
NARRATIVE WRITING UNITS

E

#1	p. 76	List, group, & label related ideas
#2	p. 77	List & group details *before* writing
#3	pp. 78-79	Organize information sequentially
#11	p. 88	Create transitions *within* paragraphs
#12	p. 89	Create transitions *among* paragraphs
#17	p. 94	Craft narrative introductions
#18	p. 95	Craft narrative conclusions
#19	p. 96	Generate titles that grab the reader

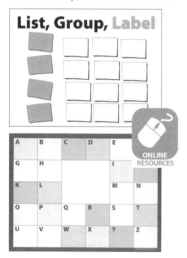
MINI-LESSON #1: List, group, & label related ideas

Logical organization is achieved when writers group related information together. Describe the organization of a grocery store where similar items are grouped in the same area (e.g., produce, dairy, frozen, meats, etc.).

A shopper doesn't expect to find a can of soup by the pet food or a bag of apples in the shampoo aisle. This is true of writing, as well. A reader expects that all information related to a facet or subtopic will be adjacent to one another in the same paragraph/paragraph block. Model how writers achieve this.

Step 1: List

• Provide a list of details about a single topic (or quickly generate one with students). Write each detail/fact on a separate sticky note.

Step 2: Group

• Read each detail aloud looking for details that "go together."
• Select 2-3 sticky notes and remove them from the board. Explain that *this, this, and this go together because they are all examples of...*
• Cluster those sticky notes together on the board.
• Look at all the remaining details to see if others fit within this same grouping. Move them accordingly.

Step 3: Label

• Label the grouping of sticky notes based on its category or what the notes have in common.

Repeat this process creating a second category (i.e., category B).

After modeling 1-2 groupings, then inquire if anyone sees another set of details that go together (i.e., category C). Repeat the list, group, and label process with the remaining sticky-note details until all have been organized into a category.

Independent Writing:

Using sticky notes, small groups generate a list of details on a new topic. (Consider concepts students have recently studied in content areas.) Then they sort the details into categories and add labels. Conclude with groups sharing their organization rationale.

MINI-LESSON #2: List & group details *before* writing

A pre-write is an organized list of key points and specific details that the writer intends to flesh out into sentences. A pre-write is essential in crafting a well-organized first draft. Without this step, a writer's ideas are presented off the cuff and haphazardly, making it hard to follow.

However, dispel the myth that pre-writing must include completing a graphic organizer. Replace this action with a simple grocery-list of details.

Describe the purpose and function of a grocery list:
- It is used by the shopper.
- Items are listed in 1-2 word phrases— not complete sentences.
- Abbreviations are used; spelling is not essential.
- It often includes numbers (to show sequence or priority) or lines/arrows (to show connection or relationship).

Describe the similar purpose and function of a pre-write:
- It is used by the writer.
- Details are listed in 1-2 word phrases— not complete sentences.
- Abbreviations are used; spelling is not essential.
- It often includes numbers (to show sequence or priority) or lines/arrows (to show connection or relationship).

Reveal shopping list paper noting that it supports the needs of both a shopper and a writer. Return to a previously-made list of details (or quickly generate a set of details on a topic). Point out that the information is abundant, but the details are unorganized.

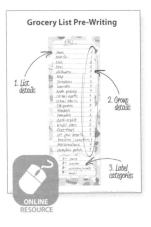

Grocery List Pre-Writing

Model how to organize the information. Read aloud the list looking for like ideas. Show the connection of similar details by linking them with lines and/or labeling them with the same number, letter, or highlighter color. Provide a category label for each grouping. (This is the same list-group-label process utilized in Mini-Lesson #1, p. 76.)

Conclude the lesson explaining that this 3-step pre-writing strategy targets both the traits of ideas and organization. First, the writer determines the relevant details and information (list). Then he organizes those ideas into logical categories (group & label).

Independent Writing:

Students create grocery-list pre-writes for multiple topics. Working with a partner, pairs create lists of details and then organize them into groups using lines, arrows, numbers, letters, or highlighter colors.

NOTE: Students do not write any first drafts on this day. They are only practicing the skill of generating organized pre-writes. Repeat this for several days, applying it to persuasive/argumentative, informative, and narrative topics.

Teacher Tip

Mini-Lessons #1 and #2 (pp. 76-77) create the foundation for pre-writing. Once students understand the general purpose and process of a pre-write, they can then apply them to any graphic organizer (e.g., *Web, Storyboard, T-Chart, Outline,* etc.).

Visual Trigger

Shopping-list or to-do list paper helps combat students' tendency to write whole sentences when pre-writing. The long skinny vertical paper supports the notion that they are creating grocery lists of details.

Teacher Tip

Mini-Lessons #1 and #2 (pp. 76-77) both apply list, group, and label in three separate steps. The difference is that Mini-Lesson #1 allows for the physical movement and manipulation of the details/sticky notes. However, Mini-Lesson #2 expects the steps to be applied on the same sheet of paper.

Teacher Tip

The *Storyboard* approach (p. 78) and the *ABC Chart* strategy (p. 79) both support the organization of sequenced information. Introduce *one* of the two strategies.

Visual Trigger

Reveal a comic strip with 5-10 frames. Identify the first frame as the "beginning," the last one as the "ending," and those in between as the "middle." Compare the chronological development of the story to the boxes in the *Storyboard* organizer.

Teacher Tip

Students can pre-write the details in simple visuals and key words without utilizing the framed boxes on the *Storyboard* organizer.

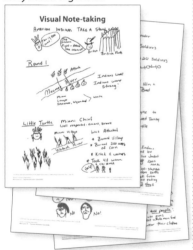

Teacher Tip

Examples of storyboards and corresponding personal narratives are accessible via the online resource.

MINI-LESSON #3: Organize information sequentially

ALL STORIES/NARRATIVES are organized chronologically. They begin with a character problem and end with a solution/resolution. Reveal a grade-appropriate anchor paper that demonstrates this chronological text structure.

SOME INFORMATIONAL TOPICS are presented in a chronological order (e.g., life cycles, historical events, biographies, systems, processes, etc.). Reveal a grade-appropriate anchor paper that demonstrates this chronological text structure.

Introduce the *Storyboard* graphic organizer.
Reveal the traditional 3-box beginning-middle-end organizer. Identify a story or concept to retell in chronological order— one detail per box (e.g., "Chip & Tomato").

Then reveal the 5-box *Storyboard* organizer (e.g., "Chip & Tomato"). Using the same topic, jot one detail per box. Repeat the process with the 9-box *Storyboard* (e.g., "Chip & Tomato"). (Middle and high school teachers may also introduce the 12-box and 15-box organizers.)

Note how much additional information unfolded in the longer versions. Compare this to writing in slow motion, capturing every relevant detail.

Explain that the 3-box version presents the middle as equivalent to the beginning and the ending. Whereas, the other versions help writers stretch out the information across the middle paragraphs.

The secret to a "meaty middle" is knowing what additional information to include. Within the *Narrative Storyboarding* and *Informative Storyboarding* handouts are suggestions for which details to reveal per box.

Independent Writing:

As a class, complete a 3-box *Storyboard* on a second event or topic. Then, pass out the 5-box organizer for students to individually stretch the middle of the same event or topic. Repeat with the 9-box *Storyboard*.

NOTE: Students do not write any first drafts on this day. They are only practicing pre-writing. Repeat this skill for multiple days.

Alternative Mini-Lesson for
Organizing information sequentially

List & organize *ABC Chart* details

Present the *ABC Chart* as a tool for sequencing information before writing. First, students recall all the facts and details (Steps 1-2). Then, they chronologically organize the information (Steps 3-5).

Model how to use the *ABC Chart* organizer.

STEP 1: Identify the topic of a recently-learned concept (e.g., water cycle) or the title of a recently read story (e.g., *Fireflies!* J. Brinkloe). Note it in the middle of the *ABC Chart*.

STEP 2: List all the information known about this topic or text. Note each detail on a sticky note and adhere it to the *ABC Chart* based on the initial letter of the detail. (Emphasize how much easier it was just to list the information without focusing on logical order, too.)

STEP 3: Near the completed *ABC Chart*, draw a graphic organizer on the board.
- For narratives, draw a large plot exposition map or *Storyboard* graphic organizer (p. 78).
- For informatives, draw a large timeline or *Storyboard* graphic organizer (p. 78).

STEP 4: Reread the sticky-note details on the *ABC Chart* looking for those that occurred at the beginning of the story or the start of the event.

STEP 5: Move the details that happened first, second, third into their appropriate positions on the organizer.

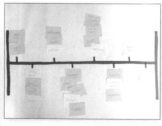

Independent Writing:

Groups complete an *ABC Chart* based on a second event, story, or topic. Then they sort the sticky notes onto the appropriate organizer. Repeat this skill for multiple days.

Teacher Tip

The *Storyboard* approach (p. 78) and the *ABC Chart* strategy (p. 79) both support the organization of sequenced information. Introduce *one* of the two strategies.

Teacher Tip

Execute this lesson with sticky notes on the ABC poster or use the digital version that works with interactive white boards. This allows the individual details to be moved into order.

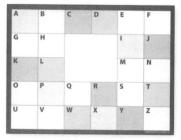

Teacher Tip

Younger and/or struggling writers tend to prefer the *ABC Chart* over the *Storyboard* organizer because it allows the writer to list *then* organize. Whereas the *Storyboard* requires writers to list *and* organize at the same time.

Teacher Tip

Clarify that students are *not* expected to have one detail per letter in Step 2. Rather, they want to recall as much information as possible. If that means there are three "R" details and zero "Q" details, that's fine. Once all details are listed, move to sequencing the information in Steps 3-5.

Follow-Up Lesson

This process is defining future paragraphs. Each grouping can be fleshed out into a topic sentence followed by its supporting detail sentences.

Teacher Tip

Many associate the *Venn Diagram* with compare-contrast writing. However, this organizer doesn't ensure comparative categories. It separates information, but it doesn't line up parallel details. The *T-Chart* is a much stronger tool for writers.

Teacher Tip

It's possible to utilize two *ABC Charts* to create compare-contrast organization. (Review Steps 1-2 from p. 79.) After listing the details about both items— one per chart— then, sort the sticky notes into comparative categories on a *T-Chart*.

Follow-Up Lessons

T-Charts organize the information within the body paragraphs. However, the content for the introduction and conclusion are not accounted for. This requires additional mini-lesson instruction (Mini-Lessons #15 and #16, pp. 92-93).

MINI-LESSON #4: Organize compare-contrast information

Compare-contrast writing requires students to juggle information on two or more ideas/items. The secret to a well-organized piece is to identify common facets relevant to both topics. This creates an apples-to-apples organization. For each subtopic compared, the writer reveals details about item A and item B and whether they are more similar or more different.

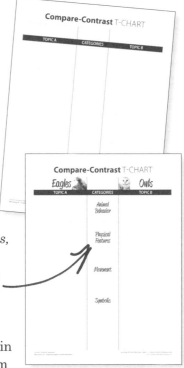

Model how to execute this with the *Compare-Contrast T-Chart*.
- Label the left and right columns with the two items being compared (e.g., *two seasons, two animals, two texts, two events,* etc.).
- List 2-4 broad categories of comparison in the middle column, keeping in mind they have to be relevant to both topics.
- Complete the chart row by row. Point out to students that the categories are broad in order to allow for multiple details per item per category.
- If the information is the same for both items, note it in both columns.

Walk students through a second *Compare-Contrast T-Chart*. Identify two concepts/items and the broad categories of comparison. (NOTE: Choose topics students know well so they can focus on organizing the information and not generating it. For example, compare two sports, two restaurants, two pets, two holidays, two foods, etc.).

Conclude the lesson revealing how the T-Chart serves as a pre-write, too. Circle each row and label it as a future paragraph. The category label can be fleshed out into a topic sentence followed by the specific supporting details for both items. Access the "Eagles versus Owls" draft via the online resource.

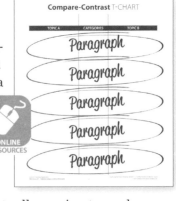

Independent Writing:

Assign another everyday topic and identify the middle-column categories. Students work in pairs to complete each row with multiple details. Repeat this skill for multiple days, eventually moving toward more complex information.

Launching the Writer's Workshop: Grades 3-12, Kristina Smekens and Maureen Scane
© 2017 Smekens Education Solutions, Inc.

Additional Resources for

Organizing compare-contrast information

Middle-column categories vary depending on the items or topics being compared. Here are some suggestions, keeping in mind all categories may not be relevant every time.

▶ When comparing a book to its movie version, focus on the story elements of both texts. Determine if the movie version stays true to the original print text.

▶▶ When comparing two characters, analyze their physical, emotional, and lifestyle differences.

▶ When comparing two literary texts (e.g., cultural versions of the same fairy tale, two texts on a similar theme, etc.), analyze how the story elements are handled in both.

▶▶ When comparing historical or sci-fi to a historical account or science textbook passage, note if the literature is an accurate representation of the factual information.

▶ When comparing two informative texts or topics, the categories of comparison are harder to determine. The secret to selecting comparable facets is based on the available information within the texts.

Teach students to read/review all the information collected from both texts and identify common components or "big ideas" for both. Remember, a compare-contrast piece requires the writer to analyze the same factors for both topics.

Follow-Up Lesson

T-Charts compare two items. However, there are instances when the writer has to juggle three or more topics:
- Compare the three branches of government.
- Compare the functions of four body systems.
- Compare the classic novel to the graphic novel to the movie version.

Convert a *T-Chart* by sliding the category column to the left and adding a vertical column for each additional topic.

Follow-Up Lesson

Persuasive and argumentative writing start with a *T-Chart*, too (Mini-Lesson #3, p. 62). However, there are sometimes more than two perspectives. For example, *Which branch of government is most important— legislative, judicial, or executive?* Or, *Which type of energy is best— wind, solar, or coal?*

Convert the *T-Chart* by labeling the top of each column with a different viewpoint and using the far left column to list the text/sources of information.

MINI-LESSON #5: Organize information categorically

Students are typically familiar with the *Web* organizer (see A below). The topic or main idea goes in the center oval. The spin-off ovals contain multiple details on smaller, related subtopics. The expectation is that each oval produces a meaty paragraph.

In concept, this organizer is great. However, students often jot only a *single* detail per oval. Then, when the ovals are filled up, they begin to draw in more single-detail ovals (see B below). This tends to produce "listy" writing, limiting the effectiveness of the traditional *Web* graphic organizer.

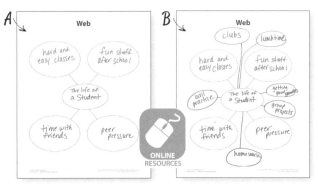

Teacher Tip

To make the concept of a *Dissected Web* easier, start with the *ABC Chart*. (Review Steps 1-2 from p. 79.)

When it's time to organize the details, sort them by like-ideas, creating a web of details.

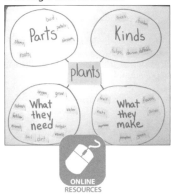

The *Dissected Web* is a stronger option (see C above). Each oval is broken into many "pieces" implying multiple details comprise a single subtopic.

Reveal an informative writing topic or recently read informational text (e.g., "How Animals 'Talk'").

1. Identify subtopics or labels for each oval based on the main idea. Note them above each oval.
2. Recall important details, relevant facts, and related vocabulary. Note them within each subtopic oval. If there are more details than "pieces," model how students can insert more lines to an oval.
3. When the *Dissected Web* is complete, explain how a writer would use it to eventually compose a first draft. Each oval represents a paragraph in the future first draft. The above-the-oval label serves as a topic sentence, and the "pieces" become the supporting detail sentences. Emphasize that the more details within the dissected oval, the more developed the paragraph will be.

Dissected Web

Follow-Up Lessons

The *Dissected Web* organizes the content of the body paragraphs. However, the introduction and conclusion are not accounted for. This requires additional mini-lesson instruction (Mini-Lessons #15 and #16, pp. 92-93).

Independent Writing:

Students work with a partner to complete a *Dissected Web* on a second familiar writing topic or text.

NOTE: Students aren't writing first drafts; they are simply practicing their pre-writing skills. Repeat this process for multiple days.

MINI-LESSON #6: Answer *what* & *why* in constructed responses

Brief constructed responses follow a *what* and *why* structure. They provide an opinion or inference (the what) and support it with proof (the why).

For those familiar with QAR (Question-Answer Relationship), constructed responses are Author & Me inferential questions. The inference is generated by the writer or "me" and supported with the author's words from the text.

A constructed response demands that the writer accomplish a lot in a few sentences. Therefore, provide students an organized formula that is efficient and versatile. The Yes, MA'AM™ acronym combines the concepts of QAR and the Test Lady™ (Mini-Lesson #5, p. 102).

Identify the function of each of the four parts of the Yes, MA'AM acronym.

- **ME**— The first sentence is the topic sentence and contains two facets. First, include a couple of key words from the original question/prompt in order to provide context for the answer. (A well-written response makes sense *without* reading the original question.) Then provide the answer, opinion, or inference to address the question. This first "ME" sentence expects the writer to reveal *what* the writer thinks.

- **AUTHOR**— The second sentence includes the *why* the writer thinks *what* he revealed in the first sentence. However, the support must come from the author/text— not the writer's personal experience or background knowledge. Use sentence starters like *The author states…, The text states…, According to the passage,…,* etc.

- **AUTHOR**— The third sentence serves the same purpose as the second sentence; it supplies a different detail from the text (e.g., *A second example from the text… The author also states…,* etc.).

- **ME**— The final sentence provides the writer's conclusion. It explains the connection between the inference and the evidence. A writer can't assume the reader understands his point. Consequently, this last sentence must: 1) restate the inference and 2) explain the writer's interpretation of it. These two facets are connected with a transition (e.g., *because, therefore, since, consequently,* etc.).

Model this formula using the *Yes, MA'AM Constructed Response* handout. Reveal a recently read text and an inferential question. Think Aloud through the four facets to create a strong response. (Multiple student examples are available via the online resource.)

Independent Writing:

Provide another inferential question based on the same text. (NOTE: Students must have access to the text.) Guide students through a Yes, MA'AM™ response.

Visual Trigger

Introduce students to the woman who writes and scores all the standardized tests— The Test Lady™ (Mini-Lesson #5, p. 102). Thus, when addressing one of "her" short-answer questions, students should generate a Yes, MA'AM™ response.

Teacher Tips

- Avoid *because* in the first sentence. Save the reasons for the second and third sentences.

- To provide context for the short response, students should name all their nouns, thus avoiding the use of vague pronouns (e.g., *he, she, it, they,* etc.).

- For more instructional ideas, read "Strategies for Short-Answer Responses" via the online resource.

Teacher Tip

Apply the facets of Yes, MA'AM within class discussions. Post the formula and/or key sentence starters to support students when composing oral responses.

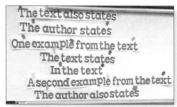

Follow-Up Lesson

Eventually, the two separate "AA" author-evidence sentences could be merged into a single one. This would be more succinct and save precious space on a standardized test.

Video Clip

For more information, watch "Adapt Yes, MA'AM to Fit Longer Essays" via the online resource.

Teacher Tip

In order for students to develop a longer written response, they need more information to work with. Consequently, the text needs to be abundant. This may be a single longer passage or multiple shorter ones.

In turn, when multiple texts are provided, the expectation is that the writer will cite evidence from *all* of the passages within the response. They cannot pull all the details from only one source.

Follow-Up Lesson

If this were an argumentative essay, the writer would include a fourth Yes, MA'AM paragraph. This one would include a counterclaim with textual evidence to support it.

Follow-Up Lesson

This lesson focuses only on the *body* paragraphs. For more information on how to craft the introduction, watch "Rework the Prompt to Serve as an Introduction" via the online resource.

MINI-LESSON #7: Adapt Yes, MA'AM™ to fit longer essays

Once students are able to generate a brief constructed response using the Yes, MA'AM™ formula (Mini-Lesson #6, p. 83), then show them how to modify it to fit longer extended-response essays.

An extended-reading response typically utilizes the five-paragraph-essay structure: introduction, three body paragraphs, and a conclusion.

Using the *Supersize Yes, MA'AM* handout, explain the difference between an extended reading response and a brief constructed response.

- The shorter writing utilizes the Yes, MA'AM formula to support a single reason or inference.
- The longer essay includes multiple inferences/reasons, each fleshed out into a separate Yes, MA'AM paragraph.

Model how to supersize a brief constructed response into an extended response. Return to a previously generated constructed response (Mini-Lesson #6, p. 83). Remind students of the original question based on the single excerpt. Provide a couple more excerpts from the same text and a revised question.

The secret to generating extended responses is to roll out information slowly. Students tend to quickly rattle off multiple reasons with a laundry list of evidence. However, the thought process isn't logical and the organization is hard to follow.

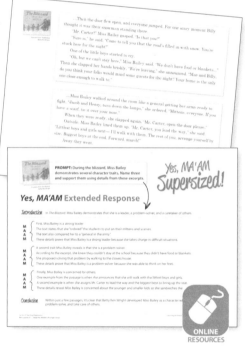

The supersized Yes, MA'AM strategy requires that each reason be introduced and explained in its own body paragraph, creating a coherent and cohesive product.

Independent Writing:

Provide students an extended-response question based on recently read text. As a class, generate a simple introduction. Then assign groups (three students per group) to write the body paragraphs. Each student in the group is responsible for writing *one* of the Yes, MA'AM™ paragraphs. (NOTE: Students must have access to the text in order to cite evidence.)

Launching the Writer's Workshop: Grades 3-12, Kristina Smekens and Maureen Scane
© 2017 Smekens Education Solutions, Inc.

MINI-LESSON #8: Reveal persuasive reasons intentionally

Return to previously generated *Two-Perspective T-Charts* (Mini-Lesson #3, p. 62). Review the process of listing reasons for both perspectives.

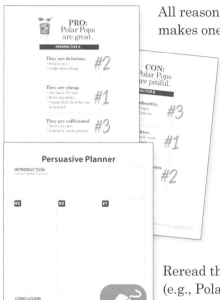

All reasons are not created equal. Define what makes one reason stronger than another.

- Strength may be determined by quantity (e.g., the reason with the most evidence is often the strongest).
- Strength may be determined by consequence (e.g., the reason with the greatest impact, the most powerful outcome, or that affects the most people may be the strong-est).
- Strength may be determined by expertise (e.g., the reason with the most experts supporting it may be the stron-gest).

Reread the list of previously generated reasons (e.g., Polar Pops are great versus Polar Pops are pitiful.). Reiterate that all reasons are not created equal. Consequently, discuss which reasons are stronger and then rank them (i.e., #1, #2, #3).

Clarify the difference between *ranking* the reasons and *presenting* them. Writers should *not* present their written reasons in the same #1, #2, #3 order. Rather, the organization should maximize reader impact. Therefore:

- Save the best (#1) for last. This ensures the final words are powerful.
- Bury the weakest reason (#3). It will likely be the shortest paragraph plunked in the middle of the more powerful ones.
- Start with the second-best reason (#2), providing a little *oomph*.

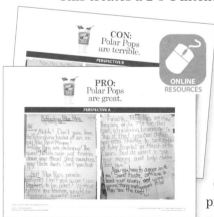

This creates a 2-3-1 intentional order. Transfer the reasons from the *Two-Perspectives T-Chart* to the *Persuasive Planner* honoring this organization. More than just having three reasons, a writer should know what his best (and weakest) reasons are so that he can present them for maximum impact. Nothing is by accident.

Reveal first drafts of the pro and con *Polar Pops* anchor papers via the online resource. (NOTE: The order these writers chose to present their reasons may not be the same sequence the students chose.)

Independent Writing:

Students reread and rank the reasons from a previous *Two-Perspective T-Chart* (Mini-Lesson #3, p. 62). They justify their rationale to a partner. After peer input, students transfer their opinion/claim and the ordered reasons to the *Persuasive Planner*.

Teacher Tip

Persuasive/Argumentative writing includes two facets— the *what* and the *why*.

- *What* does the writer think or believe? This is known as the claim, proposition, opinion, or belief and is stated clearly within the introduction.
- *Why* does the writer think or believe it? This includes the reasons and evidence detailed in the body paragraphs.

Teacher Tip

This lesson focuses on the ordering of the body paragraphs. It assumes those paragraphs are developed with statistics, facts, data, evidence, etc. For more lesson ideas on how to flesh out each reason, see Mini-Lessons #6-#13, pp. 65-72.

Teacher Tip

Access pro and con statements about genetic engineering. Choosing one side, students work in groups to sort the details into reasons, then rank them based on strength.

Follow-Up Lessons

The lesson targets the body paragraphs. However, the content for the introduction and conclusion are not accounted for. This requires additional mini-lesson instruction (Mini-Lessons #13-#14, pp. 90-91).

Teacher Tip

Access several student examples of persuasive pieces converted to arguments. All "Animal Testing" and "Bottled Water" anchor papers include black/white versions and color-coded versions to distinguish between the claims (yellow) and the counterclaims (pink).

Video Clip

For more information about this lesson concept, watch "Argumentative v. Persuasive Writing" via the online resource.

Visual Triggers

Compare the one-sided nature of the persuasive scale to the more evenly balanced argumentative scale.

Follow-Up Lesson

This lesson describes a beginner's argument. However, a more sophisticated argumentative structure is to utilize the *They say… I say…* organization (Mini-Lesson #10, p. 87).

MINI-LESSON #9: Convert a persuasive to an argument

A key difference between persuasive and argumentative writing is the acknowledgement of the opposition. Persuasive writing is one-sided. It *may* include a *brief* mentioning of an alternative perspective, but it doesn't develop it. However, an argument is a pro-con; it elaborates on both sides.

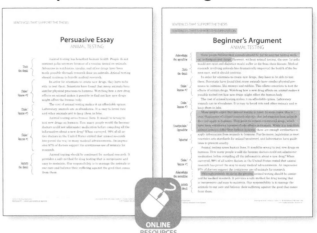

This difference is most easily seen by analyzing two pieces on the same topic.
- Reveal a persuasive writing (e.g., "Animal Testing").
- Using two highlighters, declare yellow to represent the pro-animal-testing position and pink to represent the against-animal-testing.
- Read aloud each sentence highlighting it yellow (pro) or pink (con).
- After reading, conclude that all the sentences were advocating for animal testing. There was no reference to the opposition; there was no pink.
- Read aloud the argumentative version (e.g., "Animal Testing") applying the same highlighting treatment.
- After reading, analyze the number of sentences dedicated to the opposing viewpoint. Although there are more sentences to support the thesis statement, the writer honors that the opposition has valid reasons and deserves space in the writing.

Reveal the *Beginner's Argumentative Planner* and compare it to the previously learned *Persuasive Planner* (Mini-Lesson #8, p. 85). Note the subtle, but significant differences:

- The introduction reveals the author's position *and* acknowledges the opposition.
- The body reveals the reasons/claims following the 2, 3, 1 order. However, there is a fourth body paragraph dedicated to explaining a key point for opposition (i.e., counterclaim).
- Clarify that the counterclaim's paragraph comes after the writer's weakest reason (#3) but before his strongest one (#1). This ensures the writer's perspective is what the reader hears last before concluding the piece.

Return to previous persuasive writings. Model how to convert them to arguments by referring to the opposition in the introduction, conclusion, and a single body paragraph.

Independent Writing:

Students return to a previous persuasive writing to convert it to a simple argument using a colored pen/font.

Launching the Writer's Workshop: Grades 3-12, Kristina Smekens and Maureen Scane
© 2017 Smekens Education Solutions, Inc.

MINI-LESSON #10: Present both sides of an argument

A persuasive can easily be converted to an argument (Mini-Lesson #9, p. 86) with the addition of a body paragraph. However, a more sophisticated organization includes an interior debate where the writer juggles both perspectives.

Reveal both the color-coded "Animal Testing" beginner's argument in Mini-Lesson #9, p. 86 and the color-coded "Animal Testing" anchor paper in this lesson. (The online resources are color coded to distinguish the claims from the counterclaims.)

The back and forth organization is referred to as the *They say... I say...* format. It allows both perspectives a chance to "talk" to the reader multiple times. However, this more sophisticated organization is also harder to master. The secret is found in the *Elaborate & Transition Chart.*

Model the *They say... I say...* organization.

1. Return to a previously generated *Two-Perspectives T-Chart.* (See *Polar Pops* or *ShamWow* examples in Mini-Lesson #3, p. 62.)
2. Choose one side to be the claim and the other side to be the counterclaim.
3. Starting with the thesis, complete the sentence *There are many reasons one should/should not...* Then identify a reason using the statement *One reason is...* Support that one reason with details, examples, and proof.
4. Now transition to the opposition (e.g., *On the other hand...*) and provide one reason (e.g., *One reason is...*). Elaborate with details to support it.
5. Switch viewpoints again. Transition using one of the phrases from the chart (e.g., *Even though...*), and then elaborate on a second reason supporting the claim (e.g., *Another reason...*).
6. Continue this transition-and-elaboration rhythm.

Discuss the effects of the *They say... I say...* organization.

- It allows both perspectives to weigh-in multiple times.
- The reader sees the writer as an expert because he knows so much about both sides. He appears reasonable and fair-minded.
- The piece focuses on reasons and evidence, not just voice and emotion.

Independent Writing:

The teacher facilitates an oral debate using information previously collected on *Two-Perspective T-Charts.* (See examples saved from Mini-Lesson #3, p. 62.)

- First, Partner A identifies the thesis and one reason.
- Then, Partner B transitions to the opposition and elaborates on one of its reasons.
- Continue the facilitated debate juggling claims and counterclaims.

Teacher Tip

Access several student examples that follow the *They say...I say...* format. All "Animal Testing" and "Bottled Water" anchor papers include black/white versions and color-coded versions to distinguish between the claims (yellow) and the counterclaims (pink).

Teacher Tip

During this mini-lesson and writing time, students need to see the *Elaborate and Transition Chart* in order to learn the *They say... I say...* format. Plan to provide copies of the handout and/or project it onto the screen.

Teacher Tip

Facilitate oral debates before asking students to generate anything in writing. The *Elaborate & Transition Chart* will help them master the organization before they ever write down the first sentence.

Follow-Up Lesson

Remind students that in an argument, there is always a stronger side (Mini-Lesson #3, p. 62). Therefore, although the opposition is represented throughout the draft, it shouldn't get equal space. Assess the amount of space devoted to both viewpoints by highlighting the sentences supporting the claim (yellow) versus those in support of the counterclaim (pink).

Video Clip

For more information about this lesson concept, watch "Connect Ideas *Within* Paragraphs" via the online resource.

Teacher Tip

This mini-lesson is essential once students are writing multi-sentence paragraphs. Purposeful transitions show how all the details are related. However, don't rush to teach this lesson *until* students are developing ideas with multiple supporting sentences.

Visual Trigger

Transitions are like yellow road signs alerting readers of the upcoming information. This concrete trigger is available for purchase via the online resource.

MINI-LESSON #11: Create transitions *within* paragraphs

Transitions do more than just connect ideas. They reveal how ideas within individual sentences are related to one another.

Like yellow caution signs signal to a driver the terrain to expect ahead, transitions indicate to a reader the kind of information to anticipate next. When done well, transitions move readers through a smooth journey of ideas.

Reveal the list of *Purposeful Transitions*. Explain that these are grouped in the different ways ideas/sentences can be related. Study the categories.

Just as road signs are not randomly placed, transitions shouldn't be haphazardly chosen. Reveal an anchor paper that demonstrates strong transitions between sentences (e.g, informative/ "Indian Village," persuasive/ "Babysitting," etc.). Discuss how each transition indicates how the next detail is related to the previous one. Consequently, transitions are not interchangeable. Each type reveals the unique relationship between one idea and the next.

The secret to achieving a logical flow is to determine *how* ideas are related. Model this process.

- Reveal the *Determine Relationships* handout.
- Read the first sentence and summarize its main idea.
- Read the second sentence and summarize its main idea.
- Describe how the second sentence relates to the first one (e.g., *it includes contrasting information, it adds information, it emphasizes certain information,* etc.).
- Select a transition from that category on the *Purposeful Transitions* handout, substituting it into the sentence.

Repeat the process with a second example. Then invite the students to try the next combination of sentences.

Independent Writing:

Provide additional two-sentence combinations. (These can be sentences pulled from students' previous writings or examples made up by the teacher.) Pairs work to identify the appropriate transition to join the two ideas.

(NOTE: The focus of this activity is for students to think about the sentence content and talk about the relationship of information. Expect students to justify their transition choices.)

Launching the Writer's Workshop: Grades 3-12, Kristina Smekens and Maureen Scane
© 2017 Smekens Education Solutions, Inc.

MINI-LESSON #12: Create transitions *among* paragraphs

Not only should individual sentences within a paragraph be connected (Mini-Lesson #11, p. 88), but entire sections of the piece should also flow logically. To guide the reader from one major point/paragraph to another, writers craft a strong transition sentence.

Reveal the blended colors of variegated/multi-colored yarn. The blue section blends into the purple section with a blue-purple segment. This is what a transition sentence should do, too. Its purpose is to gently merge the reader from one paragraph (blue) to the next (purple), connecting the ideas between them with a transition sentence (blue-purple).

Model how to create a smooth transition sentence using the "House" description.

- Read aloud the first paragraph and determine its main idea.
- Then read and summarize the main idea in the second paragraph.
- Brainstorm multiple sentences that connect the two paragraphs.
- Select the strongest transition sentence.
- Read the third paragraph. Summarize its content and how it relates to the second/previous paragraph.
- Brainstorm transition sentences connecting paragraphs two and three.
- Continue modeling this process.

Present the *Blend Paragraphs* handout. Challenge students to generate transition sentences between each of the two-paragraph combinations.

Independent Writing:

Students return to a previous piece separating paragraphs using story surgery (Mini-Lesson #2, p. 33). Provide strips of colored paper and have them reassemble the writing, taping a colored strip between each paragraph. Challenge students to write transition sentences on the colored strips connecting the different paragraph blocks.

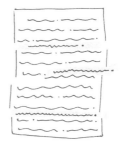

Launching the Writer's Workshop: Grades 3-12, Kristina Smekens and Maureen Scane
© 2017 Smekens Education Solutions, Inc.

Teacher Tip

All the documents supporting this mini-lesson are color-coded to support the concept of blended sentences.

Visual Trigger

Multi-colored yarn shows that the two colors are connected with a blended section. This parallels the idea of a transition sentence blending two paragraphs.

Teacher Tip

This lesson is best executed after students are developing paragraphs with multiple sentences and staying on topic (Mini-Lesson #15, p. 74).

Teacher Tip

Be sure to offer a variety of transition possibilities. Don't imply that there is a single right answer.

Mentor Text

Find multiple anchor papers that include color-coded transition sentences within the online resource.

Teacher Tip

This writing task can be executed digitally, as well. Students return to a previously typed draft and change the font to make each paragraph a different color (e.g., ¶1 red, ¶2 blue, ¶3 green, ¶4 black, etc.). Then, they insert blended transition sentences that include colors from both paragraphs. (Another option is to change the font or size of the text per paragraph, too.)

Mentor Text

Several student examples of persuasive and argumentative introductions are available via the online resource.

Teacher Tip

Here is an instructional scaffold in line with grade-level writing standards.

GRADE 3— State the opinion/thesis + Allude to the reasons

GRADES 4-5— Provide background information + State the opinion/thesis + Broadly reference the reasons

GRADE 6— Provide background information + State the opinion/thesis + Explicitly state the reasons

GRADES 7-12— Provide background information + Acknowledge the opposition + State the opinion/thesis + Explicitly state the reasons

Visual Trigger

Introductions are made up of multiple "pieces" of information.

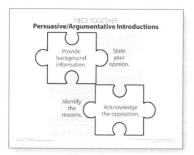

JPEGs of puzzle-piece graphics are available via the online resource.

MINI-LESSON #13: Craft persuasive/argumentative introductions

There is no recipe for writing an introduction. Rather, there are lots of possible pieces or ingredients that could be arranged to craft a strong opening. The focus of this mini-lesson series is to introduce the combination of sentences that often comprise a persuasive/argumentative introduction that are grade-appropriate (see Teacher Tip).

NOTE: The content in this mini-lesson likely spans multiple days. Plan to introduce the facets of the introductory paragraph, explaining their purposes and revealing examples.

- **Provide background information on the topic/text.** A writer cannot assume his readers know anything about this topic. Therefore, before making a claim, he must educate his reader. This includes a sentence or two to introduce the topic and explain the purpose of the piece. This might include leading with a hard-hitting fact, describing a scenario, or defining key vocabulary. If the piece is about a literary text, then provide a 1-2 sentence summary of the plot.

- **State the opinion, position, belief, or proposal within a thesis statement** (Mini-Lesson #2, p. 61). This sentence summarizes the main idea of the entire piece.

- **Acknowledge an alternative perspective.** An argument mentions the opposition early in the introduction. It typically utilizes an opening phrase like *Opponents believe… Some say…* or *A common belief is….*

- **Identify the reasons.** The writer identifies why he believes his thesis/opinion is right. These reasons are represented within the introduction in one of three ways: 1) Explicitly state each reason (e.g., *Wearing school uniforms eliminates peer pressure, reduces morning stress, and saves families money.*). 2) Broadly reference the reasons to be identified in the body paragraphs (e.g., *Wearing school uniforms reduces emotional, personal, and financial pressure.*). 3) Allude to reasons in general (e.g., *Students should want to wear school uniforms for three reasons.*).

Using a previous writing, model how to craft an introductory paragraph using strips of paper (i.e., sentence strips).
- Include background information on one or two sentence strips.
- (Argument only) Acknowledge the opposition on another strip.
- Utilize a final sentence strip to write the opinion/thesis and reference the reasons.

Begin to arrange and rearrange the sentence strips to come up with the best sounding combination. Tape together the final product. (NOTE: Transition words and phrases may be added to link sentences together.)

Independent Writing:

Using a previous piece, students write out each sentence of the introduction on a sentence strip. Then they arrange and rearrange the sentences to come up with the best combination and tape them together.

Launching the Writer's Workshop: Grades 3-12, Kristina Smekens and Maureen Scane
© 2017 Smekens Education Solutions, Inc.

MINI-LESSON #14: Craft persuasive/argumentative conclusions

There is no recipe for writing a conclusion. Rather, there are lots of possible pieces or ingredients that could be arranged to craft a strong closing paragraph/section. The focus of this mini-lesson series is to introduce the combination of sentences that often comprise a persuasive/argumentative conclusion.

NOTE: The content in this mini-lesson likely spans multiple days. Plan to introduce the facets of the concluding paragraph/section that are grade-appropriate (see Teacher Tip).

- **Restate the opinion, position, belief, or proposal.** Reiterate the opinion but do so in a slightly different way. Use synonyms to create a variation of the thesis statement. (In a book or movie review, this statement often includes a rating— 3 stars, 2 thumbs-up.)

- **Acknowledge the opposition.** If writing an argument, the ending must again acknowledge what "others" say. However, reference the opposition early in the conclusion. This gets it out of the way, reserving the final words for the writer's position.

- **Remind the reader what's at stake.** Don't summarize the reasons within the conclusion. (The standards do not require a summary ending.) Rather, demonstrate the consequences if the reader does not agree with the writer. This sentence is often referred to as the *So What?* or *Consider this* statement. Think beyond the piece; identify the impact or predict an outcome if the writer's viewpoint isn't accepted. This sentence often adds drama and/or tugs at the reader's heartstrings.

- **Reveal a call to action.** Some topics require the reader to demonstrate agreement by taking action. This may include telling the reader to do something, to stop doing something, to say something, to stop saying something, to buy something, to try something, etc. This sentence gives the reader direction; it challenges him to take action.

- **Finish with a clever one-liner.** A witty statement, a unique twist, or a play on words can make for a memorable last line. Although it's not a requirement, such a one-liner sticks with the reader.

Using a previous writing, model how to craft a concluding paragraph using strips of paper (i.e., sentence strips).
- Restate the opinion/thesis on one sentence strip.
- (Argument only) Acknowledge the opposition on another strip.
- Remind the reader what's at stake on a sentence strip.
- (If applicable) Identify a call to action on a sentence strip.
- (If possible) Craft a clever one-liner.

Begin to arrange and rearrange the sentence strips to come up with the best sounding combination. Tape together the final product. (NOTE: Add transition words and phrases as needed.)

Independent Writing:

Using a previous piece, students write out each facet of the conclusion on a sentence strip. Then they arrange and rearrange the sentences to come up with the best combination and tape them together.

Mentor Text

Several student examples of persuasive and argumentative conclusions are available via the online resource.

Teacher Tip

Here is an instructional scaffold in line with grade-level writing standards.

GRADES 3-4— Restate the opinion/thesis + Reveal a call to action

GRADES 5-6— Restate the opinion/thesis + Reveal a call to action &/or Remind the reader what's at stake

GRADES 7-12— Acknowledge the opposition + Restate the opinion/thesis + Reveal a call to action &/or Remind the reader what's at stake + Finish with a clever one-liner

Visual Trigger

Conclusions are made up of multiple "pieces" of information.

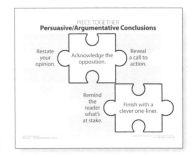

JPEGs of puzzle-piece graphics are available via the online resource.

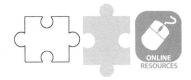

Mentor Text

Several student examples of informative introductions are available via the online resource.

Video Clip

For more information, watch "Piece Together Informative Introductions" via the online resource.

Teacher Tip

Here is a suggested scaffold in line with grade-level writing standards.

GRADES 3-4— Provide background information + Identify the narrow topic

GRADES 5-6— Provide background information + Define important words/concepts + Identify the narrow topic

GRADES 7-12— Provide background information + Define important words/concepts + Identify the narrow topic + Convey the importance

Visual Trigger

Introductions are made up of multiple "pieces" of information.

JPEGs of puzzle-piece graphics are available via the online resource.

MINI-LESSON #15: Craft informative introductions

There is no recipe for writing an introduction. Rather, there are lots of possible pieces or ingredients that could be arranged to craft a strong opening. The focus of this mini-lesson series is to introduce the combination of sentences that often comprise an informative introduction.

NOTE: The content in this mini-lesson likely spans multiple days. Plan to introduce the facets of the introductory paragraph(s) that are grade-appropriate (see Teacher Tip).

- **Provide background information on the topic/text.** Don't assume the reader knows anything about this topic. Therefore, before revealing the thesis statement, the writer has to educate his reader. Take a sentence or two to introduce the broader subject matter. If the piece is about a literary text, then provide a 1-2 sentence summary of the plot. If the piece is a compare-contrast of two items, then the writer needs to provide a general explanation or description of both items.

- **Identify the narrow topic.** The thesis statement (Mini-Lesson #2, p. 61) reveals the narrow scope of the subject matter. This sentence identifies the specific facets that will be covered in the piece.

- **Introduce important words/concepts.** Informative writing is often about specialized concepts or unfamiliar topics. The reader needs a general understanding of the subject matter before diving deeply into the piece. Within a sentence or two, provide a key-word definition, a concept explanation, or a real-life comparison to build some background knowledge for the reader.

- **Convey the importance of the topic.** The reader may know a little about the topic but doesn't understand its importance. Communicate the severity of the subject with a startling fact. Hook the reader with a powerful expert quote. Point out relevancy with a vignette describing those impacted. Any of these strategies sets a tone of importance; they get the reader to pay attention.

Using a previous writing, model how to craft an introductory paragraph using strips of paper (i.e., sentence strips).
- Include background information on one or two sentence strips.
- Introduce important words or concepts on another sentence strip.
- Write the thesis statement on a single sentence strip.
- Utilize a final sentence strip to convey relevance/importance.

Begin to arrange and rearrange the sentence strips to come up with the best sounding combination. All options do *not* have to be used. Transition words and phrases may be added to link sentences together. Tape together the final product.

Independent Writing:

Using a previous piece, students write out each facet of the introduction on a sentence strip. Then they arrange and rearrange the sentences to come up with the best combination and tape them together.

Launching the Writer's Workshop: Grades 3-12, Kristina Smekens and Maureen Scane
© 2017 Smekens Education Solutions, Inc.

MINI-LESSON #16: **Craft informative conclusions**

There is no recipe for writing a conclusion. Rather, there are lots of possible pieces or ingredients that could be arranged to craft a strong closing paragraph/section. The focus of this mini-lesson series is to introduce the combination of sentences that often comprise an informative conclusion.

NOTE: The content in this mini-lesson likely spans multiple days. Plan to introduce the facets of the concluding paragraph that are grade-appropriate (see Teacher Tip).

- **Restate the thesis or main point.** In a single sentence, connect the ending to the beginning by reiterating what the piece was about. Use synonyms and a slightly different sentence structure to create a variation of the thesis statement. However, repeat *only* the thesis— not all the reasons. (The standards do not require a summary ending. Teach other options for the conclusion to beef up this final paragraph.)

- **Identify the end result.** Some topics naturally end with an outcome (i.e., what was gained, learned, realized), a result (i.e., an effect or by-product), or an update (i.e., the current status). Provide this new information in the conclusion.

- **Offer some good news.** Reveal the advantages of this topic, the benefits of this situation, or an interesting fact about this concept. Such a final sentence offers the reader a silver-lining perspective— a little hope or encouragement. This is especially powerful if the topic was negative, harsh, severe, or just all around heavy.

- **Return to a previous statement.** Circle back to an earlier part of the writing where a scene was described or a quote was stated. Reference the original and update it. Identify the impact or implications the subject had on people and/or places. This is referred to as a loop ending.

Using a previous writing, model how to craft a concluding paragraph using strips of paper (i.e., sentence strips).
- Restate the topic sentence/thesis statement on a sentence strip.
- (If applicable) Identify the end result on a sentence strip.
- (If applicable) Provide a good news or silver-lining statement on a sentence strip.
- Return to a previous statement and update it on a sentence strip.

Begin to arrange and rearrange the sentence strips to come up with the best sounding combination. All options do *not* have to be used. Transition words and phrases may be added to link sentences together. Tape together the final product.

Independent Writing:

Using a previous piece, students write out each facet of the conclusion on a sentence strip. Then they arrange and rearrange the sentences to come up with the best combination and tape them together.

Mentor Text

Several student examples of informative conclusions are available via the online resource.

Video Clip

For more information, watch "Craft Informative Conclusions" via the online resource.

Teacher Tip

Here is a suggested scaffold in line with grade-level writing standards.

GRADES 3-4— Restate the thesis + Identify the end result

GRADES 5-6— Restate the thesis + Identify the end result + Offer some good news

GRADES 7-12— Restate the thesis + Identify the end result + Offer some good news + Return to a previous statement

Visual Trigger

Conclusions are made up of multiple "pieces" of information.

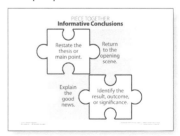

JPEGs of puzzle-piece graphics are available via the online resource.

MINI-LESSON #17: Craft narrative introductions

There is no recipe for writing an introduction. Rather, there are lots of possible pieces or ingredients that could be arranged to craft a strong opening. The focus of this mini-lesson series is to introduce the combination of sentences that often comprise a narrative introduction.

NOTE: The content in this mini-lesson likely spans multiple days. Plan to introduce the facets of the introductory paragraph(s) that are grade-appropriate (see Teacher Tip).

- **WHAT: Establish the situation.** Identify the character's problem, conflict, wish, want, need, or goal. Whether this is done with intense action, emotional dialogue, or a declarative sentence— the reader needs to know the character's plight. A story requires a problem. There has to be a conflict that is resolved by the end.

- **WHO: Introduce the character(s).** Give the reader someone to care about. Describe what the character looks like, how the character feels, who the character is related to, what role the character plays in the story, etc. Whether providing some or a lot of specifics, reveal only the character details that the reader *needs* to know.

- **WHEN & WHERE: Describe the setting.** Describe where the character is. Explain where the action is happening. Orient the reader with basic time, date, and/or geographic location information. Sensory details, weather details, and mood details add sophistication. Reveal only the setting details that are relevant to the characters or the problem.

Using a previous writing, model how to craft an introductory paragraph using strips of paper (i.e., sentence strips).
- Create 1-2 sentence strips about the situation (i.e., what).
- Create 1-2 sentence strips about the characters (i.e., who).
- Create 1-2 sentence strips about the setting (i.e., when & where).

Begin to arrange and rearrange the sentence strips to come up with the best sounding combination. Reveal various combinations:
- Identify the setting, then the characters, followed by the problem.
- Start with the situation to build intrigue and motivate the reader to continue reading in order to get some answers. After a few sentences of the "what," then back up and lay the "who" and "where" foundation.
- Describe the main character. Then zoom out and show the character within a particular setting. Then zoom out further and establish the greater context or situation that reveals the problem.

Show several combinations. Transition words and phrases may be added to link sentences together. Tape together the final product.

Independent Writing:

Using a previous piece, students write out each facet of the introduction on a sentence strip. Then they arrange and rearrange the sentences to come up with the best combination and tape them together.

Mentor Text

Several student examples of narrative introductions are available via the online resource.

Teacher Tip

Here is an instructional scaffold in line with grade-level writing standards.

GRADES 3-4— WHAT/Establish the situation

GRADES 5-6— WHO/Introduce the character(s) + WHAT/Establish the situation

GRADES 7-12— WHO/Introduce the character(s) + WHEN & WHERE/Describe the setting + WHAT/Establish the situation

Visual Trigger

Introductions are made up of multiple "pieces" of information.

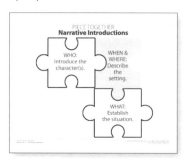

JPEGs of puzzle-piece graphics are available via the online resource.

Launching the Writer's Workshop: Grades 3-12, Kristina Smekens and Maureen Scane
© 2017 Smekens Education Solutions, Inc.

MINI-LESSON #18: Craft narrative conclusions

There is no recipe for writing a conclusion. Rather, there are lots of possible pieces or ingredients that could be arranged to craft a strong closing paragraph. The focus of this mini-lesson series is to introduce the combination of sentences that often comprise a narrative conclusion.

NOTE: The content in this mini-lesson likely spans multiple days. Plan to introduce the facets of the concluding paragraph that are grade-appropriate (see Teacher Tip).

- **Fix-up.** Writing guru Barry Lane breaks stories into three chunks— set-up (beginning), mix-up (middle), and fix-up (ending). A narrative conclusion *begins* when the climax is over. Describe the final action or event. Within a sentence or two, reveal how the problem was fixed or resolved. (NOTE: This might include a surprise or twist ending.)

NOTE: Although the basic plot is over in the "fix-up" sentence(s), these are often abrupt endings. Compare them to Hallmark Channel or Lifetime television movies. These entire movies are consumed with the conflict and rising action. Then, the final five minutes includes the climax, the presumed happily ever, and then the credits roll. This is okay; it's technically a narrative since it had a problem and resolution, but... it's lacking a wrap-up (see below).

- **Wrap-up.** Don't end the story after the final action or event. Rather, tie up loose ends. Bring the story full circle with a description of how things look now. Explain the status of characters and their feelings. Advance time a few days, weeks, or months past the final action or event. Describe life after "the end."

- **Look-up.** With the problem now resolved, step out of the story and reflect on it. Step back and see the bigger picture. Describe the lesson learned (e.g., theme, moral). Explain the significance or importance of the story. Provide a clever or witty final thought. Offer a personal comment about life. This is the writer's opportunity to offer the reader his 20/20 hindsight vision. Think of this like the *If I knew then what I know now...* sentence.

Using a previous writing, model how to craft a concluding paragraph using strips of paper (i.e., sentence strips).
- Create 1-2 sentence strips about the fix-up.
- Create 1-2 sentence strips about the wrap-up.
- Create 1-2 sentence strips about the look-up.

Begin to arrange and rearrange the sentence strips to come up with the best sounding combination. All options do *not* have to be used. Transition words and phrases may be added to link sentences together. Tape together the final product.

Independent Writing:

Using a previous piece, students write out each facet of the conclusion on a sentence strip. Then they arrange and rearrange the sentences to come up with the best combination and tape them together.

Mentor Text

Several student examples of narrative conclusions are available via the online resource.

Teacher Tip

Stories require problems to be identified in the beginning and solutions reached by the end. Consequently, a writer needs to have the introduction (Mini-Lesson #17, p. 94) and conclusion (p. 95) planned *before* he fleshes out the body paragraphs.

Teacher Tip

Here is an instructional scaffold in line with grade-level writing standards.

GRADES 3-4— Fix-up

GRADES 5-6— Fix-up + Wrap-up

GRADES 7-12— Fix-up + Wrap-up + Look-up

Visual Trigger

Conclusions are made up of multiple "pieces" of information.

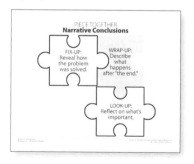

JPEGs of puzzle-piece graphics are available via the online resource.

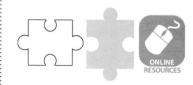

Visual Triggers

Wrap three boxes or access the images below via the online resource.

ONLINE RESOURCES

Teacher Tip

Using the internet, search for book titles under a particular topic (e.g., shark attack). Simply right-click on the cover images to save each as a JPEG. These can serve as example titles within the mini-lesson.

Mentor Text

Don Wulffson's *The Kid Who Invented the Popsicle* is a great resource for 100 short, high-interest nonfiction passages that each include a label but need a title. Purchase this text via the online resource.

Follow-Up Lesson

Connect this lesson to the temporary titles students used to stay on topic in a first draft (Mini-Lesson #15, p. 74). Students eventually return to the title to revise and customize it for the specific content inside.

MINI-LESSON #19: Generate titles that grab the reader

Titles are like the bow atop a gift package; they are the first thing the reader sees. Present three identically wrapped boxes with three different toppers (see Visual Triggers). *Which would you rather receive?*

Point out the differences among the three bows and compare them to titles.

- A present without any adornment (e.g., ribbon, bow, etc.) implies the giver doesn't think too highly of what's inside. Similarly, a piece without any title implies the writer doesn't think too highly of what's inside.
- A present with a bow that's been used over and over is like a title that is used over and over by many students. If the title can be applied to anybody's writing, then it's nothing special (e.g., "Summer Vacation," "Chapter Summary," "Persuasive Essay," etc.).
- A present with a unique and customized bow demonstrates the special attention it was given. A lot of thought went into the gift wrapping and likely what's inside, too. Similarly, writers communicate the same sentiment with a specialized, customized, attention-grabbing title.

Reveal several titles on the same topic (e.g., shark attack).

- Discuss the different impressions of each title.
- Discuss what students like/dislike about each.
- Compare the titles of these texts to a more generic one (e.g., *Shark Attack*). Point out how that same "bow" could be the title to any of the books because it's so generic.
- Return to the stronger titles and note how they are specialized and customized to the unique content to come.

Reveal the *Types of Titles* handout. Study the different impressions they each give. Then model how to try on different titles for the same piece using *Try On Titles* handout.

- Reveal a text with a generic title (e.g., "Hot Dog").
- Generate multiple titles and consider the strengths and weaknesses of each.
- Compare this process to trying on different gift bows to determine which one best matches the color, the proportion, the effect, etc.

Independent Writing

Provide another text with a generic title. (Multiple short texts are available via the online resource.)

Partners generate several title options and mark their favorites. Or, students return to a previous piece, write three titles, and mark their favorites.

Teaching Voice

Voice seems to be a more ambiguous trait. It's possible to point to ideas and details, see the introduction, body, and conclusion, and compliment specific word choice. But voice tends to be more abstract.

When a piece has voice, the author's purpose and perspective are clear. When the voice is strong, the reader feels connected to the writer and/or the piece.

However, voice is often a misunderstood trait. Voice goes far beyond the writer's personality. Although voice seems to come naturally to some writers more than others, it can be explicitly taught and cultivated in everyone. Voice is depicted in words the writer chooses, and yet it's different than the trait of word choice.

Voice is a choice. Provide students opportunities to experiment with various writer attitudes based on the purpose, audience, and topic.

Trait-Based Mini-Lessons

Mini-lessons for
PERSUASIVE & ARGUMENTATIVE WRITING UNITS

#1	p. 98	Detect and name the voice
#3	p. 100	Infuse voice in 3 ways
#4	p. 101	Choose voice based on the P.A.T.
#5	p. 102	Introduce the Test Lady™
#6	p. 103	Maintain a respectful tone in arguments
#7	p. 104	Combine perspective and POV

Mini-lessons for
INFORMATIVE WRITING UNITS

#1	p. 98	Detect and name the voice
#3	p. 100	Infuse voice in 3 ways
#4	p. 101	Choose voice based on the P.A.T.
#5	p. 102	Introduce the Test Lady™
#7	p. 104	Combine perspective and POV

Mini-lessons for
NARRATIVE WRITING UNITS

#1	p. 98	Detect and name the voice
#2	p. 99	Show actions, don't tell feelings
#3	p. 100	Infuse voice in 3 ways
#4	p. 101	Choose voice based on the P.A.T.
#7	p. 104	Combine perspective and POV

Teacher Tip

Broaden students' vocabulary of feeling words. Generate a list of attitudes and include a student photo expressing each one.

Mentor Text

...for Emotions & Attitude

The Blue House Dog, D. Blumenthal
The Dot, P. Reynolds
Ish, P. Reynolds
Fireflies! J. Brinckloe
The Harmonica, T. Johnston
The Memory String, E. Bunting
The Relatives Came, C. Rylant
Testing Miss Malarkey, J. Finchler
The Wall, E. Bunting

Follow-Up Lessons

Voice is relevant in all types of writing— narrative, informative, persuasive, argumentative. Eventually move beyond the feelings and mood of narrative writing to the more sophisticated application of voice in informative, persuasive, and argumentative. Within these follow-up lessons, clarify that the trait of voice serves a different purpose.

• In informative writing, the confident and authoritative voice makes the reader listen and learn from the writer.

• In persuasive writing, the passionate and powerful voice convinces the reader.

• In argumentative writing, the objective and formal tone demonstrates the writer is fair-minded.

MINI-LESSON #1: Detect and name the voice

Voice is the writer's attitude about the topic. Just like individuals can change hairstyles, enjoy various ice cream flavors, or select music based on their moods, voice is a choice. For every topic, a writer determines how he feels about it and then conveys that attitude, tone, or voice to his reader.

Pieces that lack voice— voiceless writing— are mechanical. There is no attitude detected, no perspective reflected. It's all about the information and just getting it onto the paper. The writer comes across as indifferent, uninvolved, and distant from both the topic and his reader. These pieces are stale and boring.

Reveal examples of voice-rich text. (There are several student writing samples available via the online resource, or see Mentor Text suggestions.)

Model how to detect and name the voice.

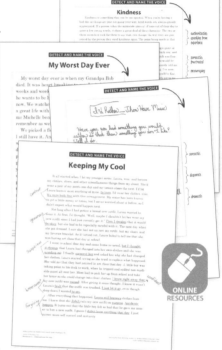

• Reveal a voice-rich writing sample or excerpt from mentor text.
• Read aloud a paragraph or so.
• Reread the paragraph and underline the words and details that reveal voice, feeling, and attitude.
• Note in the margin a feeling word or emotion that captures the sentiment or tone of these details.
• Identify this as the "voice."
• Read aloud the next portion and repeat the modeling.
• Discuss the power the writer possesses to set the tone or voice through the words and details he chooses to use.
• Point out that the same piece often shifts voices throughout. It does not have to maintain the same attitude from start to finish.

Independent Writing:

Provide recently read texts/excerpts in a variety of modes/genres. (Excerpts used in *Recognizing Voice in Literature* handout are from middle and high school literature.) Pairs/groups list the voice(s) they hear within each excerpt and the words/phrases that indicate that attitude.

(NOTE: This writing-time task has students reading like writers. They are identifying the author's perspective based on evidence in the text.)

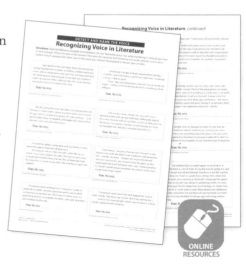

Launching the Writer's Workshop: Grades 3-12, Kristina Smekens and Maureen Scane
© 2017 Smekens Education Solutions, Inc.

MINI-LESSON **#2: Show actions, don't tell feelings**

Encourage students to "show" feelings and attitude, rather than "tell" them to the reader. Instead of stating a character is *sad*, show the reader what sad looks like. Describe the character's *head hanging down, face frowning, tears rolling down cheeks, lips trembling,* etc.

The secret to showing rather than telling is to identify the close-up details that capture a feeling. Model how to dramatize a feeling. Act out the mannerisms, gestures, and facial expressions of a nervous person (e.g., *biting nails, twisting hair, fidgeting, looking at the clock repeatedly, sighing heavily,* etc.).

Once students guess the feeling (e.g., nervous, worried, anxious), ask them to list the "clue details" that helped them draw that conclusion. Note these "showing" details on a wall chart.

Act out a second secret emotion (e.g., feeling sick or ill). Students infer the feeling and identify the "showing" details. Emphasize that the "showing" details are *not* synonyms; they are descriptions. The list includes strong action verbs, specific adjectives, and precise nouns that capture what the feeling looks like when acted out.

Model how these "clue details" then become the basis for descriptive sentences in the writing. Generate a 2-3 sentence "showing" description for nervous and another one for feeling ill.

Clarify that this skill is not "show *and* tell." It means that writers never actually reveal the feeling word (e.g., *nervous, worried, anxious, feeling sick, ill,* etc.). The visual image is so clear the reader infers it.

Announce a third feeling (e.g., *furious*). This time have students stand up and act out what furious looks like. Encourage them to look around at their classmates while they are holding their own poses. After a few minutes, collect the "show" details the students observed.

Independent Writing:

Assign small groups several different emotions from the *Show, Don't Tell* handout. Groups act out the different feelings and then list the "showing" details. Expect 4-6 action phrases to describe each emotion. For an added challenge, students then use the "clue details" as the basis for a 2-3 sentence "showing" description.

Or, students return to previous drafts and revise "telling" sentences into "showing" descriptions.

Mentor Text

...for Show, Don't Tell
Come On, Rain! K. Hesse
The Blue House Dog, D. Blumenthal
Fireflies! J. Brinckloe
The Memory String, E. Bunting
Old Coyote, N. Wood
Polar Express, C. Van Allsburg
The Relatives Came, C. Rylant
Saturdays and Teacakes,
   L. Laminack
Taste of Blackberries,
   D. Buchanan Smith

Mentor Text

The power of body language, facial expressions, and hand gestures is evident in some State Farm Insurance commercials. The exact same words are spoken by two characters, but the feelings are quite different. View the commercials and generate "showing" details that fit the different attitudes.

Follow-Up Lesson

Writers don't physically act out every feeling their characters have. Rather, they close their eyes and visualize the scene. Based on that depiction, they generate a list of "showing" details to use within their descriptive sentences.

Video Clip

The content and word choice of a message changes its meaning. For a video example, see "Word Connotations Convey Tone" via the online resource.

Teacher Tip

Download a list of social studies vocabulary that is organized into positive and negative word connotations.

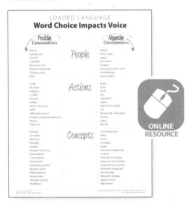

Follow-Up Lesson

Students will each choose a topic and read aloud their entries for the *Awww…* Contest. The winner is the one who earns the loudest "awww" from the students. Students should infuse a combination of content, word choice, and presentation to maximize the voice potential.

MINI-LESSON #3: Infuse voice in 3 ways

Students can "show" character feelings within stories/narratives (Mini-Lesson #2, p. 99). However, voice is part of informative, persuasive, and argumentative pieces, as well. Among the reasons, evidence, facts, and details, writers intentionally infuse voice in three ways. (While revealing the three strategies below, reference the examples within the *Loaded Language* handouts.)

1. **Reveal specific content.** The details and information the writer reveals about the topic says a lot about how he feels. For example, when writing about the beach, if the intended mood is relaxation, then point out the rhythmic sound of waves and gentle breeze. However, if the attitude is one of frustration, then describe the rambunctious, too-close "neighbors" that stretch out their blanket nearby. Writers decide which details to include in order to paint the appropriate picture in the reader's mind.

2. **Choose loaded words.** Scrutinize the word choice. It's not just *what* the writer says (content) but *how* he says it (word choice). This is where a large vocabulary serves a writer well. Precise language more clearly conveys voice. For example, the term *deal,* as in *made a deal,* is a generic reference to a historical event. However, saying that one group *bribed* or *ripped-off* the other indicates the writer's attitude about the "deal." These precise words each contain a different connotation, and thus voice.

3. **Present the information.** Consider how to present the information. Font, style, color, size, punctuation, illustrations, etc. each carry a connotation. When an author italicizes a word, capitalizes an entire word, makes a word bold, or adds an exclamation mark— he is indicating emphasis. Compare this to the use of emojis in text messages. The sender's attitude may be unclear based on the content alone. However, the emoji lets the reader know just how he feels.

Reveal informative and persuasive/argumentative anchor papers that communicate voice through a combination of content, word choice, and format. Multiple examples are available via the online resource. NOTE: All three techniques do *not* have to be used simultaneously.

Independent Writing:

Assign a quick write topic (e.g., field trip to an area museum). Students generate a first draft making content, word choice, and format decisions to convey a precise attitude (e.g., a mundane or boring museum field trip). Write another draft that communicates a different perspective (e.g., a surprisingly fabulous museum field trip). Revise for a third attitude (e.g., an exhausting museum field trip). Conclude with a brief discussion on the power an author possesses in determining the voice or tone of the piece.

MINI-LESSON #4: Choose voice based on the P.A.T.

Voice is the writer's attitude about the topic, but how does the writer choose his voice? How does he know what attitude to convey? That's the focus of this mini-lesson.

Inquire if students have ever seen a book where each page is divided into thirds and the reader can create different combinations of heads, torsos, and legs. Reveal the flap book graphic and what each flap represents.

Choose Voice based on the **P.A.T.**

> Purpose
> Audience
> Topic

- **P— Purpose** = *Why you're writing* (e.g., to inform, to persuade, to entertain, etc.).
- **A— Audience** = *To whom you are writing.*
- **T— Topic** = *What you are writing about.*

Just like those character flap books, the writer can create any combination of purposes, audiences, and topics. And depending on those choices, the writer's voice will emerge. Read three short descriptions on the *Choose Voice* handout. Even though the topic is the same for all three (e.g., a food fight), the different purposes and audiences generate different voices/writer attitudes.

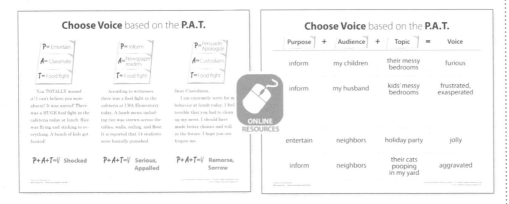

Reveal the completed *Choose Voice* chart. Identify the writing topic (e.g., T = children's messy bedrooms). Then, point out the P and A columns. Reveal the what V that combination would likely create. Keeping the same topic (T), change the audience (A). That will likely impact the purpose (P) and the voice (V), too.

Show the same process, but start with the audience (e.g., A= my neighbors). Identify the topic (T= neighborhood holiday party), the purpose (P) and the likely voice (V). Then, maintain the same audience but change the topic (e.g., T= cats pooping in my garden). Determine the appropriate purpose and voice.

Writers choose their voice (V). But, it's based on why they're writing (P), to whom they're writing (A), and what they're writing about (T).

Independent Writing:

Using the *Choose Voice* chart, identify a topic and then various audiences. Then change it up. Identify one audience but various topics to write to them about. NOTE: Students are not writing sentences or any drafts. They are simply playing with combinations of P.A.T. that impact V.

Teacher Tip

Model topics and/or audiences students cannot "steal." Using *spouses* as the audience or *parenting* as the topic would be great models to demonstrate the lesson skill, but not ones that students could simply copy.

Follow-Up Lesson

These four facets are typically determined as part of the pre-writing process. Eventually, require students to identify the P+A+T, and thus the V *before* they begin their next pieces.

Mentor Text

...for Test Lady™ Audience
Hooray for Diffendoofer Day!
  Dr. Seuss
Testing Miss Malarkey, J. Finchler

Video Clip

During the 2010 Literacy Retreat, the Smekens Education staff participated in a Test Lady™ Style Show. Each Test Lady represented an essential component in strong prompt response. Their demeanor, clothing, props, and/or accessories mirrored their favorite parts of good writing.

Follow-Up Lesson

Connect this concept of the Test Lady to the woman reading the Yes, MA'AM constructed responses (Mini-Lesson #6, p. 83).

Follow-Up Lesson

Rather than drawing the Test Lady, students could find a photo to represent her. This particular example was chosen to be the Test Lady by a fourth grade class. They named her Vestibule McFlannery.

MINI-LESSON #5: Introduce the Test Lady™

To provide students a stronger sense of audience, the scorers behind the state writing assessments need to be humanized. Giving students a person to write to is more motivating than if they think their writing will be scored by a machine. This is what prompted Kristina Smekens to invent the Test Lady™, the person who reads and scores all the standardized tests, including the constructed responses, extended reading responses, and essays to writing prompts.

Knowing there is a human being on the other end makes it a more authentic experience and consequently more motivating to write. This impacts the writer's attitude and thus his voice.

Add a little mystery and intrigue with The Test Lady lesson. Although various teachers have spoken with her by phone (about what she looks for in "good writing" on state assessments), no one has actually seen her. Reveal examples of *Test Lady Portraits* drawn by students.

Be sure to describe the Test Lady™ as kind. She is eager and enthusiastic to read the students' writings. (Don't make her an old, bitter woman who hates her job. Who would want to write to that person?)

Identify the Test Lady early in the school year. When students write about texts they've read, topics they've discussed, or concepts they've learned, remind them to write their responses to the Test Lady. Since she wasn't in the classroom during any of the instruction/discussion, students naturally provide more specifics. They begin to realize the importance of restating part of the question in order to provide her some much needed context. The concept of the Test Lady provides students with an authentic audience.

Independent Writing:

Students generate portraits of the Test Lady™ as they visualize her (and they can identify writing goals, too).

Display the students' Test Lady portraits within the room. Remind students of their Test Lady audience before they take any standardized reading/writing assessment.

Launching the Writer's Workshop: Grades 3-12, Kristina Smekens and Maureen Scane
© 2017 Smekens Education Solutions, Inc.

MINI-LESSON #6: Maintain a respectful tone in arguments

A big difference between persuasive and argumentative is how voice is addressed. Persuasive writing often includes a powerful and passionate attitude. It's clear how the writer feels about the topic.

However, the writer's voice in argument is more objective. It's a controversial subject that's already charged with emotion. Therefore, the argument is based on careful thinking and powerful evidence. Arguments still have voice, but it's a more formal tone. Reveal the "Do" column on the *Maintain a Respectful Tone* chart.

In addition to presenting the claim with reasons and evidence, arguments also acknowledge the opposition. While fleshing out one or two reasons in support of the counterargument, the writer must remain respectful. This attitude goes a long way in convincing the reader. If the writer shows consideration for other viewpoints, he reveals he is well informed and rational in his thinking. These characteristics can go a long way in convincing readers.

ARGUMENTATIVE WRITING
Maintain a Respectful Tone

Do!

…explicitly state your reasons.

…provide abundant and relevant facts, evidence, and statistics.

…cite experts who agree with you.

…reference the opposing side's argument and refute their claims.

…use passionate language and be sincere.

Don't!

…present a reason with *I believe, I feel* or *I think*—just say it!

…claim to be an expert.

…sound superior, condescending, or impolite when referencing the opposition.

…disrespect or belittle the opposition's beliefs (e.g., *You're dumb if you think…*).

…use absolute statements (e.g., *always, forever, every time,* etc.).

ONLINE RESOURCE

As important as knowing what to do, it's essential to know what not to do in an argumentative piece. Reveal the "Don't" column on the *Maintain a Respectful Tone* chart.

- Don't disrespect or belittle the opposition's beliefs (e.g., *You're dumb if you think…*).
- Don't sound superior, condescending, or impolite when referencing the opposition.
- Avoid absolute statements (e.g., always, forever, every time, etc.).

None of these techniques scores points with a reader. In an argument, the writer doesn't woo with voice and feeling. He convinces the reader with logical reasoning and an objective tone.

Independent Writing:

Return to a previous argumentative writing. Revise to meet the expectations described on the *Maintain a Respectful Tone* chart.

Mentor Text

...for First-Person Point of View

All the Places to Love, P. MacLachlan
Because of Winn-Dixie, K. DiCamillo
Come on, Rain! K. Hesse
Diary of a Worm, D. Cronin
Lawn Boy, G. Paulsen
Love That Dog, S. Creech
Owl Moon, J. Yolen
The Polar Express, C. Allsburg
Smoky Night, E. Bunting
The True Story of The 3 Little Pigs!
    J. Scieszka
The Wall, E. Bunting

Teacher Tip

Students often jump between second and third-person POVs. Students need instruction on how to rework their writing so that *you* is not the subject of their sentences.

Follow-Up Lesson

Although it's easier to reveal perspective/voice within first-person writing, most pieces utilize a more formal third-person POV. See Mini-Lesson #3, p. 100 for ways to infuse voice within informative, persuasive, and argumentative writing.

Follow-Up Lesson

Identify a recently studied person or topic (e.g., slaves fleeing via the Underground Railroad, the functions of a cell, the life cycle of a chick, the process of digestion, etc.). Assign students to write with voice/perspective from that subject's first-person point of view. (Multiple content-area writing samples are available via the online resource.)

ONLINE RESOURCES

MINI-LESSON #7: Combine perspective and POV

Review that voice is the attitude, feeling, or perspective the writer has about a topic (or a character has about a situation). Perspective is the *how* the writer/character feels.

Point of view is the *who*— who is telling the details or providing the information. Often pieces are written in a third-person POV.

- **Third-Person POV** uses the pronouns *he, she, it, they, them,* etc. The writer is the narrator telling *about* the thoughts, feelings, perspectives, tones, and attitudes of more than one person/character.

However, there are times when the writer can take on the persona of someone else *and* the perspective or voice that comes with it.

- **First-Person POV** uses *I, me,* or *we*. These pieces are told from the main character's perspective; the author *is* the main character. In this writing, the author cannot reveal other character's thoughts or feelings; he only knows of his own. (See Mentor Text for examples.)

Model how to write about the same topic/situation from multiple points of view and with different perspectives. Reveal a photograph with multiple "characters." Generate a third-person description of the scene. Write it on the top of the *Perspective Versus Point of View* handout.

Then, identify 3-4 different points of view ("characters") represented within that topic, issue, or scene. Write each one within the 1, 2, 3, 4 boxes of the *Perspective Versus Point of View* handout.

Generate a first-person description of the same scene for every "character" in the image.

- *What would the dog be thinking/feeling?*
- *What would the boy be thinking/feeling?*
- *What would the mom be thinking/feeling?*
- *What would the dad be thinking/feeling?*

Reinforce that students can write *about* characters using the third-person POV, or they can write *as if they are* the characters using first-person POV. Although writers can choose, the key is to remain consistent throughout the piece. In other words, the same "character" reveals the information throughout the whole piece. (NOTE: Multi-perspective books are exceptions, where every chapter/section is told from a different character's point of view and thus presents a different voice or perspective.)

Independent Writing:

Using the *Perspective Versus Point of View* handout, identify a topic (e.g., passing period) or issue (e.g., bullying in school) or a photo (e.g., kids eating in the lunchroom). In addition, identify 3-4 different points of view ("characters"). Students generate a quick write for each POV (i.e., *who* is providing the details/information) revealing an appropriate attitude, perspective, or voice (i.e., *how* they feel).

Teaching Word Choice

Strong word choice comes down to using the right word in the right spot; it's bullseye writing. Teach students how to select precise synonyms, while avoiding overused words. Beyond specific nouns and descriptive adjectives, focus heavily on action verbs. These make the greatest impact in achieving rich language.

Trait-Based Mini-Lessons

P	#1	p. 106	Choose the right word for the right spot
I	#2	p. 107	Energize writing with strong action verbs
E	#3	p. 108	Eliminate dead/retired verbs
	#4	p. 109	Minimize helping and linking verbs
	#5	p. 110	Weave in close-up details

Visual Trigger

Compare shades of crayons to shades of words. Students need to pull from a vocabulary of 64-box crayon words rather than settling for the 8-box crayon choices.

Video Clip

Celebrate rare word choice with the stroke of the purple highlighter. Watch "Got Purple Words?" via the online resource for an explanation of the purple-word procedure.

Teacher Tip

After reading informational text, have students retell facts and key details using terms from the index or select vocabulary from the passage.

Follow-Up Lesson

Including expert vocabulary is important but so is reader understanding. Teach students how to follow domain-specific terms with definition details to support reader comprehension (Mini-Lesson #6, p. 65).

MINI-LESSON #1: Choose the right word for the right spot

Writers attempt to select the perfect words to craft every sentence of their writing. The more exact the word choice, the more likely the reader will fully comprehend the message. However, students often settle for generic words that are "good enough" to convey the gist.

GENERIC WORD CHOICE:
The dog ran across the street.

PRECISE WORD CHOICE:
The mangy, white dog scampered across the alley.

ONLINE RESOURCES

The secret to choosing the right word for the right spot is understanding the power of synonyms. Synonyms are *not* words that mean the same thing. They are shades of words. Just like choosing the most precise shade of red lipstick, pink nail polish, yellow wall paint, or blue shirt, there are many different choices. Most people tend to toil over the various shades. If they select a color that's off just a little, they are dissatisfied. This is how writers work, too. Words come in various shades. Many students settle for the generic *blue* word, not considering the more precise shades of *periwinkle, indigo, navy, royal,* or *cornflower.*

Like color shades, synonyms are all subtly different from each other. A generic word (e.g., *mad*) does not conjure up an exact image for the reader. However, if the writer chose *disappointed, upset, frustrated,* or *furious,* the reader would have a much clearer understanding of just how mad the character/author is. Synonyms each have their own distinct meaning.

This is obviously applicable in descriptive/narrative writing but also in informative writing. Utilizing domain-specific vocabulary conveys a level of expertise. Each vocabulary term has its own precise definition; complex words have complex meanings. Composing sentences with expert language communicates more precise information to the reader.

GENERIC VOCABULARY:
Some people think it's bad to try out new medicines on animals.

EXPERT VOCABULARY:
Animal advocates argue it's cruel to inject untested medicines on lab rats, monkeys, and rabbits.

ONLINE RESOURCES

Clarify that this is *not* a lesson about making sentences longer or stringing adjectives together. In fact, the "expert" sentence above is stronger mostly due to the precise noun and verb choices.

Model how to brainstorm such bullseye vocabulary. Reread a previous draft and identify a sentence that includes vague nouns, imprecise adjectives, and/or a generic verb. Rework it to communicate the exact meaning intended.

Independent Writing:

Students reread previous drafts, identifying sentences that lack bullseye vocabulary. Revise word choice to include exact nouns, precise verbs, and specific adjectives.

Launching the Writer's Workshop: Grades 3-12, Kristina Smekens and Maureen Scane
© 2017 Smekens Education Solutions, Inc.

MINI-LESSON #2: Energize writing with strong action verbs

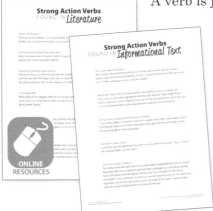

A verb is just like the battery in a remote control. It makes the sentence move. It makes the nouns move. It creates all of the action. Consequently, when choosing verbs, look for the most high-powered, energized ones— not a weak "dollar-store" verb.

Reveal mentor text excerpts with strong action verbs. Consider weaker verbs the author *could* have chosen.

Reveal an age-appropriate photograph. Using it as the "topic," list a variety of *weak* verbs related to the image. For example:

- The girl *gets* a strawberry.
- She *puts* it into the fountain.
- She *makes* it extra chocolatey.
- She *gets* some on the tablecloth.

Then brainstorm strong verbs for the same photograph.

- The girl *selects* a strawberry.
- She *pokes* it into the fountain.
- She *coats* it with more chocolate.
- She *drips* some onto the tablecloth.

Reveal another grade-appropriate photo. With the students participation, generate a list of action verbs depicted within the scene. (Several images are available via the online resource.)

When brainstorming slows down, identify a different subject observable in the same image.

Independent Writing:

With a partner, students generate lists of action verbs based on additional photos provided.

PIE

Visual Triggers

Like a battery within a TV remote, the verb is the power or engine of any sentence. If the nouns create the pictures in the reader's mind, then verbs make those pictures move.

Teacher Tip

Consider images, photos, diagrams, and other visuals that correspond with concepts learned in science and social studies (e.g., Native Americans, body systems, planets, etc.). Listing action verbs for those images would target word choice *and* serve as content review.

Follow-Up Lesson

Action verbs should be a part of the first draft, not something saved for revision. However, students tend to pre-write only nouns and adjectives associated with the topic. If brainstorming precise topic-related verbs became part of their process, it would ensure stronger word choice within first drafts.

Visual Trigger

The R.I.P. tombstone or a retired jersey number represent the forever nature of "dead" verbs.

Teacher Tip

Conduct this lesson *without* opening a thesaurus. Students know lots of verbs, but they often settle for the first one they think of. When pushed, they can typically think of a stronger synonym without the aid of outside resources.

Teacher Tip

The notion of burying or retiring words is not new to many teachers. However, it's often relegated to adjectives (e.g., *fun, cool, awesome, nice,* etc.) and nouns (e.g., *stuff, things,* etc.). Be sure to conduct a separate mini-lesson on tired and overused *verbs*.

Teacher Tip

The ABC Chart is a useful tool for brainstorming alternatives. Put the overused word in the middle and generate more precise options within the letter boxes.

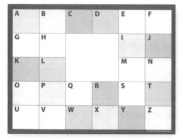

MINI-LESSON #3: Eliminate dead/retired verbs

Some words are weak because they are overused. Others may be weak because they are vague. But some words are both— overused and vague! When those words are verbs, they should be eliminated. If the verb is the engine to the sentence, then it must be powerful and precise.

Identify the most overused and vague verbs that students tend to use (e.g., *get/got, go/went, did/do, make/made, take/took, put,* etc.).

The reason these verbs are so weak is that each of them constitutes so many different possibilities. *How did you "get" it? Steal it, sneak it, snatch it, grab it, purchase it, contract it?* The context of the sentence will determine the most appropriate "get" verb. It's more than just replacing the verb with a set of choices. Writers have to reread the piece and determine which verb most precisely captures the action.

Reveal the *Get Outta Here* handout. As a class, brainstorm synonyms for "get" that would fit the context of each sentence. (For an extra challenge, avoid repeating any verbs.)

Spend a few minutes having students flip through their own previous writings to assess how often they see this dead/retired verb in their own pieces.

Point out the synonyms for *get/got* that they have generated within the *Get Outta Here* handout. Conclude the lesson by building a wall chart that will list the dead or retired verbs. Write *get/got* on the chart.

Independent Writing:

Identify additional verbs students need to bury/retire (e.g., *take/took, make/made, put, go/went, did/do,* etc.). Pairs use the short passages (available via the online resource) to identify more precise verbs. Then bury/retire the original ones by adding them to the wall chart.

Eventually, students revise previous pieces replacing the dead/retired verbs with stronger ones.

MINI-LESSON #4: Minimize helping and linking verbs

When emphasizing action verbs, simultaneously limit the number of linking and helping verbs students utilize.

Reveal a writing sample that includes strong *word* choice, but weak *verb* choice (e.g., "Autumn"). Identify the precise words that are powerful (e.g., *giddy children, brittle leaves, earthy aroma, gooey perfection, crimson leaves,* etc.). Point out that these are adjectives and nouns. Then, list the weak verb choices (e.g., *have, goes, is,* etc.).

Identify these as helping and linking verbs and mark every one with a heavy black **X**. Count how many **X**s are on the page. The boldness of those dark, black **X**s really stands out!

Model how to revise the sentences to eliminate or replace the helping/linking verbs with strong action verbs. This may include:

- Substituting the helping verb/verb with a single action verb (e.g., ~~are baking~~, bake).
  - Restructuring the sentence to eliminate the linking verb, adding in a new powerful action verb (e.g., *Trees ~~are sad~~. Trees shiver and sigh.*).
- Adding descriptive detail to the sentence (e.g., *The moon ~~is~~ behind a cloud. The moon peeps out behind a cloud.*).
- Replacing a weak phrase for a single, stronger action verb (e.g., *The moon ~~is high above~~..., The moon governs...*).

Reveal the revision (e.g., "Autumn"). Conclude the lesson with an additional key instructional point: A piece with only action verbs is not necessarily the goal. Too much information all the time creates very dense sentences. It's common for a writer to include an occasional linking verb to provide some relief for the reader.

Independent Writing:

Students select a previous draft and mark each helping and linking verb with an **X**. Announce how many helping/linking verbs can be in their revision (e.g., *You can use up to three helping and / or linking verbs. All others must be substituted, replaced, or revised.*) Be sure to identify ways that students can make room for these revisions (Mini-Lesson #2, p. 33).

Teacher Tip

This lesson can be tied to writing more efficient sentences (Mini-Lesson #5, p. 116).

MINI-LESSON #5: Weave in close-up details

An author uses his word choice to create a reader's visualization. In order to achieve this, the writer must provide powerful and precise close-up details.

Project two similar images (e.g., two monsters). Be sure the images are *more similar* than they are different. Then read a short description about *one* of the images, asking students to identify which image the passage is referencing.

After students select the "answer" image, discuss the details that were most helpful in their decision-making (e.g., *flawless skin, teeth of varying lengths,* etc.). Note that without those close-up details, they would not have known which image was correct. Explain that had the author used vague description (e.g., *a scary monster, gross teeth, black eyebrows, gloved hands,* etc.), students would not have known which image was being referenced. This is the kind of precision and close-up details students need to include within their writing.

Model how to craft a close-up-detail description.

- Reveal another set of similar images (e.g., two vases of flowers). If students are ready for more of a challenge, provide them three similar-looking images.
- Identify which of the images will be "the answer" (e.g., Image #2).
- Create a list of general descriptive phrases that is true for both/all of the images (e.g., *several yellow sunflowers, displayed in clear vase,* etc.).
- Study the images more carefully. Look for something that makes Image #2 different than the other(s). List the details unique to the "answer" image only.
- Weave together a short description that includes details relevant to both/all images and those precise ones applicable to only "the answer."

Independent Writing:

Students play *Guess the Image*. Provide students with two similar photographs. Students secretly select one to be the "answer" and list details relevant to both scenes in the left column. Then, they focus on what makes the "answer" image unique, listing those close-up details in the second column. Students generate a quick write to read aloud to their peers.

Teacher Tip

Acquire photographs using the "images" tab of any search engine (e.g., Google "vase of flowers" or "pool party").

Bell-Ringer Idea

Once students know how *Guess the Image* works, this can be a morning-work or bell-ringer activity.

Follow-Up Lesson

Strong description includes knowing what *not* to do. Clichés are overused phrases. Identify these so students know to avoid them and instead utilize fresh images.

Teaching Sentence Fluency

SECTION 12

Sentence fluency is measured by the overall readability of a piece— how easily the reader can "get through" it the first time.

To improve sentence fluency, first, provide students a way to assess their current sentence-length variety. Then explain how and when to include short and long sentences within narrative, informative, persuasive, and argumentative writing. Teach students to recognize and incorporate parallel structure to add a final layer of sophistication to their writing.

Trait-Based Mini-Lessons

Mini-lessons for
PERSUASIVE & ARGUMENTATIVE WRITING UNITS

#1	p. 112	Assess sentence-length variety
#3	p. 114	Vary sentences based on information
#4	p. 115	Add sophistication to persuasive sentences
#5	p. 116	Create long *and* efficient sentences
#6	p. 117	Add rhythm with parallel structure

Mini-lessons for
INFORMATIVE WRITING UNITS

#1	p. 112	Assess sentence-length variety
#3	p. 114	Vary sentences based on information
#5	p. 116	Create long *and* efficient sentences
#6	p. 117	Add rhythm with parallel structure

Mini-lessons for
NARRATIVE WRITING UNITS

#1	p. 112	Assess sentence-length variety
#2	p. 113	Apply fluency in narrative writing
#5	p. 116	Create long *and* efficient sentences
#6	p. 117	Add rhythm with parallel structure

MINI-LESSON #1: Assess sentence-length variety

One characteristic of strong sentence fluency is varied sentence length. When sentences are similar in length, the piece has a numbing sameness. Strong writing includes an occasional short or long sentence amid the medium-length ones. Define a short sentence as being 1-5 words and a long sentence as being more than 10 words. Everything else is considered medium.

With an understanding of what constitutes short, medium, and long sentences, assess the sentence-length variety of an anchor paper (e.g., original versions of "Winter Tunnels" or "Stealth").

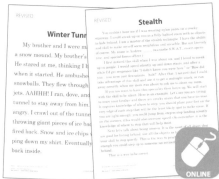

• Read the piece aloud, applying punctuation as indicated by the author. (Students might move their arms or stretch Slinkies per sentence while the teacher reads aloud.)
• Note that the piece is grammatically and mechanically correct. However, the overall sound of the writing is nothing special; it has a numbing sameness to it.
• Count up the number of words per sentence, noting them within the *Charting Fluency* handout.
• Label each sentence small (S), medium (M), or large (L) in the third column.

Read the revised writing (e.g., revised versions of "Winter Tunnels" or "Stealth"), applying punctuation as indicated by the author. (Students might again move their arms or stretch their Slinkies per sentence.)

• Note the number of words per sentence and the S, M, or L label on the *Charting Fluency* handout.
• Compare the overall sound and charted sentence-length variety of the original piece to that of the revision. How is the mood different between the two versions?
• Acknowledge that medium-length sentences are necessary in order to appreciate the drama of the other two lengths.

Clarify that a piece can be conventionally correct and still weak in sentence fluency. This trait is about the sound of the writing— not the look of it.

Independent Writing:

Assess the sentence-length variety of multiple short pieces previously written (or single paragraphs from a longer piece). Provide a separate *Charting Fluency* handout per writing. Students are *not* revising; they are only assessing.

MINI-LESSON #2: Apply fluency in narrative writing

Sentence-length variety is not just about including long and short sentences. It's about placing information in the right-sized sentences to create the greatest impact for the reader. This mini-lesson addresses intentional sentence length applied to narrative writing.

Identify the information to reveal in short sentences. Read the *Original* and *Revised* versions of "Running Late." Despite the same information revealed in both examples, discuss the impact of the second version with its shorter sentences. Point out how the same details were chopped up to create short, staccato sentences.

Short sentences in narratives:
- Convey intensity or energy.
- Relay a fast-paced scene.
- Establish an angry tone or mood.
- Depict a sense of urgency or emergency.

Identify the information to reveal in long sentences. Read the *Original* and *Revised* versions of "At the Beach." They provide the same information, although presented in different sentence lengths. Discuss the differences. Point out how the same details were merged to craft a long, lingering sentence.

Long sentences in narratives:
- Establish a quiet, calm, or peaceful moment.
- Describe slow-motion action.
- Capture a bored or mundane mood.
- Reveal character thoughts or insights.

Introduce the combination of short-short-short-long sentences. Often, several short sentences are followed by a longer one that reflects on or concludes the "fast" facts or actions. Reveal this with mentor text or anchor papers (e.g., excerpt from *Fox*, Margaret Wild or "Winter Tunnels").

A whole story of short sentences would be annoying and a whole story of long sentences would be endless. The dramatic effect works best when short and long sentences are used together. Review the key points of this lesson within the *Apply Fluency in Narrative Writing* handout.

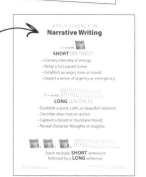

Independent Writing:

Students return to previously written narratives and revise an excerpt that would benefit from shorter sentences and an excerpt that would sound better if stretched into longer sentences.

Teacher Tip

Be sure to project the text revealed within this mini-lesson. Students need to see the sentence lengths while appreciating the sound of the sentence fluency.

Mentor Text

...for Fast v. Slow Topics
An Angel for Solomon Singer, C. Rylant
Be Kind to Eddie Lee, V. Fleming
Fox, M. Wild
Night Running, E. Carbone
A River of Words, J. Bryant
Smoky Night, E. Bunting
Twilight Comes Twice, R. Fletcher
Walter the Farting Dog, W. Kotzwinkle

Bell-Ringer Idea

Practice writing intentionally long or intentionally short sentences as a morning-work or a bell-ringer activity. Each day, assign one "fast" and one "slow" quick-write topic for students to experiment with.

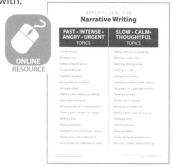

Follow-Up Lesson

Dialogue in narratives tends to be boring because it's written in complete sentences. However, natural sounding dialogue is characterized by short fragments and long ramblings. Ironically, these make narrative writing *more* sophisticated. (See "Stealth" and an excerpt from *Wonder,* R.J. Palacio via the online resource.)

MINI-LESSON #3: Vary sentences based on information

Sentence-length variety is not just about including long and short sentences. It's about placing information in the right-sized sentences for the greatest reader impact. This mini-lesson addresses sentence lengths appropriate for informative, persuasive, and argumentative writing.

Identify the information to reveal in longer sentences.

- Introduce the topic/thesis sentence.
- Explain reasons or thinking.
- Clarify data or facts reported.
- Restate/Summarize a previous point.
- Conclude a thought or reason.

Identify the information to reveal in shorter sentences.

- Isolate hard-hitting facts in their own short sentences.
- Punctuate an idea in a short, declarative sentence.
- Restate a previous point in a short, succinct sentence.
- Add voice in a short, witty sentence.

A whole piece of short sentences would be annoying and a whole piece of long sentences would be endless. Within individual paragraphs, look to offer the reader a mixture.

Model how to create this variety. First, list information on a recently learned topic. Then craft a long topic sentence with several shorter detail sentences and a final longer concluding sentence.

The sentence fluency is best when short and long sentences fit the information being presented.

Independent Writing:

Students return to a previously written informative, persuasive, and/or argumentative piece. They revise paragraphs to improve sentence-length variety.

Launching the Writer's Workshop: Grades 3-12, Kristina Smekens and Maureen Scane
© 2017 Smekens Education Solutions, Inc.

MINI-LESSON #4: Add sophistication to persuasive sentences

NOTE: Teach Mini-Lesson #3, p. 114 *before* this series of lessons. Once students have mastered when to varying sentences length, then execute this mini-lesson for an added layer of sophistication.

NOTE: The following skills would be introduced across multiple mini-lessons.

- **Declare, announce, or demand in a short sentence.** Powerful statements tend to fizzle in long sentences. If more explanation is necessary, precede or follow the short sentence with a longer one.

- **Utilize imperative sentences to avoid using "you."** Most informative and argumentative writing is formal, omitting the second person reference. Get around this with an imperative sentence implying the subject is "you" the reader, but not literally stating it.

- **Repeat information for drama and impact.** With every mention of the same word, phrase, or sentence, it escalates in power. Consider repeating an idea if the information is important, the phrasing is witty, or the impact is severe.

- **Use an em dash to interrupt a thought.** Placed anywhere in the sentence, an em dash abruptly announces important information, makes a key point, or offers a distinct contradiction.

- **Itemize information using a colon.** Colons indicate to readers a list, a quote, or an important statement will follow. If written in a parallel structure (Mini-Lesson #6, p. 117), these lists can add fluency and efficiency (Mini-Lesson #5, p. 116). When info is provided in a list, most articles (e.g., *a, an, the*) and conjunctions (e.g., *and, also*) can be omitted, tightening up the sentence.

- **Share background information within parentheses.** Writers may offer the reader a little background information or provide some added context for an idea. Rather than stating it within a traditional sentence, the writer whispers it as an aside using a set of parentheses. This is the writer's way of saying *You may already know this, but I'm giving a little extra info in case you didn't.*

Independent Writing:

Students return to a previously written informative, persuasive, and/or argumentative piece. They revise sentences to incorporate some of these sophisticated sentence structures.

MINI-LESSON #5: Create long *and* efficient sentences

As students attempt to create longer sentences, they often add words but not information. Teach the difference.

Although long sentences include more words, there should be no filler or fluff. Every words counts. Long sentences are *not* just short sentences stretched out with more words. Longer sentences must include more information. That's the notion of efficient writing.

Reveal examples depicting long and *inefficient* versus long and *efficient*.

ORIGINAL:	LONG & INEFFICIENT:	LONG & EFFICIENT:
He got a broom.	He went over and got a broom that he could then use.	He ran over, dug through a pile, and found a broom.

Point out that the original sentence had four words. The first revision stretched it to 12 words, but the reader learned nothing new. It is *inefficient*. The efficient revision only requires 11 words and yet provides so much more detail. Label the second revision as long and efficient.

If something is efficient, then it maximizes productivity with the least amount of effort. Therefore, efficient writing maximizes the information using the fewest words. Reveal a second example.

ORIGINAL:	LONG & INEFFICIENT:	LONG & EFFICIENT:
It rained a lot yesterday.	It was very wet and really rainy all day long and all night long yesterday.	Yesterday it misted most of the morning, drizzled on and off in the afternoon, and thunder-stormed throughout the night.

Reveal *7 Strategies to Lengthen Sentences*. Then, identify which strategies were used in the two examples above. Note that it's possible to utilize more than one strategy in each sentence.

Reveal additional sentences and guide students through various ways to lengthen them while *also* adding information for the reader. (NOTE: Show students how to combine two or three strategies.) Original sentences:

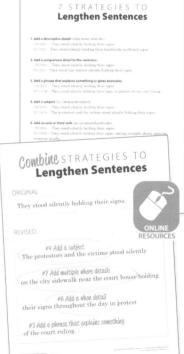

The girl found the money.	The ground shook.
The boys played football.	The pizza was cheesy.
His sister is short.	The team cheered.

Independent Writing:

Provide a list of short sentences and long/inefficient counterparts. Students stretch each one, applying various techniques from the *7 Strategies to Lengthen Sentences* handout.

Follow-Up Lesson

Announce that the class will be participating in a single-sentence writing contest. The winning sentence (as judged by someone outside of the class) is the one that best captures the season with efficient descriptive writing.

During writing time, students will walk the school grounds, gather inspiration, and generate a single-sentence contest entry. This may be a two-day activity.

NOTE: Students are disqualified for generating a run-on sentence.

 Examples of student entries are available at "Fall-Walk Sentences" via the online resource.

Follow-Up Lesson

Longer sentences tend to produce run-ons. Coordinate this lesson with instruction on grammar (e.g., compound sentences, complex sentences, etc.) and mechanics (e.g., commas/conjunctions, semi-colons, etc.).

Launching the Writer's Workshop: Grades 3-12, Kristina Smekens and Maureen Scane
© 2017 Smekens Education Solutions, Inc.

MINI-LESSON #6: Add rhythm with parallel structure

Parallelism— writing in word patterns— is a major contributor to strong sentence fluency. Introduce this technique using baby snap-beads. Three red beads snapped together represents a noun, noun, noun pattern. A blue-red pattern of beads represents an adjective-noun, adjective-noun, adjective-noun pattern.

Explain that items in a series should be presented in the same pattern, meaning each item between the commas should utilize the same part(s) of speech. Reveal examples within the *Single-Sentence Parallelism* handout.

Then reveal a non-parallel sentence and characterize it with colored beads that do *not* create a pattern (e.g., red (noun), blue-red (adjective-noun), and green (prepositional phrase). Emphasize that although a sentence can be mechanically correct, it doesn't sound *fluent* or smooth. There is no rhythm to it.

To create parallelism with items in a series, the writer first selects one structure from those in the list and then revises all the others to create the same word pattern.

ORIGINAL:
At the grocery, we bought green grapes, a bunch of bananas, and apples.

REVISION:
At the grocery, we bought green grapes, yellow bananas, and red apples.

Reiterate that there is no correct pattern. In fact, return to the same original sentence and revise it again using a different structure.

SECOND REVISION:
At the grocery, we bought a container of grapes, a bunch of bananas, and a bag of apples.

Repeat this process with a second nonparallel sentence.

ORIGINAL:
After ball practice, I'm going to eat something, take a long hot shower, and sleep.

REVISION:
After ball practice, I'm going to eat, sleep, and shower.

SECOND REVISION:
After ball practice, I'm going to eat a big filling meal, take a long hot shower, and sleep for several uninterrupted hours.

Walk students through the revision process for parallel structure using the "Lunch" and "Sleepover" passages.

Independent Writing:

Students reread previous drafts, identifying sentences that are nonparallel. They rewrite each one, creating two different parallel structures using the *Experiment with Parallelism* template.

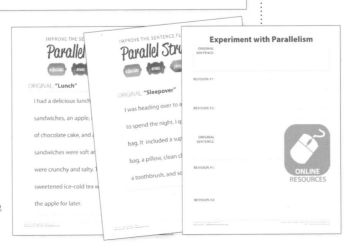

Visual Trigger

Use plastic baby snap-beads to demonstrate the idea of creating word patterns.

Mentor Text

...for Parallel Structure
In November, C. Rylant
Jake's 100th Day of School, L. Laminack
Piggie Pie! M. Palatini
The Recess Queen, A. O'Neill
The Relatives Came, C. Rylant
The Sandman, R. Fletcher
The Sunsets of Miss Olivia Wiggins, L. Laminack

Teacher Tip

Students can also use colored pens or highlighters to represent different parts of speech. This way they can self-assess that they are creating parallel word patterns within their sentences.

Launching the Writer's Workshop: Grades 3-12, Kristina Smekens and Maureen Scane
© 2017 Smekens Education Solutions, Inc.

Teaching Conventions

SECTION 13

Conventions are the tools and rules writers use to make their messages more clear for readers. To support students' mastery of grammar and mechanics, teach conventions within the context of the students' own writing. Grammar taught in isolation often produces students who can "fix" practice sentences on worksheets but cannot apply those same skills within their own writing.

Instructional Insights

Trait-Based Mini-Lessons

Define the two facets of conventions

CONVENTIONS = GRAMMAR + MECHANICS
Rules of writing   *Tools of writing*

Conventions has two parts: grammar and mechanics. Grammar represents words, phrases, parts of speech, usage, sentence types, and sentence structure. Mechanics includes the tools writers use within and among sentences. These are end marks, inner-sentence punctuation, capitalization, spelling, word spacing, margin spacing, and paragraph indents.

Conventions are unspoken agreements between readers and writers. Writers follow the rules and use the tools so readers can fully grasp the intended message.

Writers need conventions when composing the original message. Depending on the meaning of the message, the writer can state *I'm SO thirsty!* or *I'm......soooooooooooooooooooo.......thirsty!*

These two sentences have different meanings. Consequently, the application of grammar and mechanics is different.

Teach conventions in context

This requires teaching and applying conventions during the drafting stage— not saving it as a facet of editing only. Conventions are chosen based on the context of the message.

When conventions are taught in the context of real, authentic writing, then classroom instruction would *not* look like the list on the left but rather possess the characteristics of the one on the right.

Best Practice!

Correcting in isolation.	**Composing in context.**
• Instruction utilizes anonymous sentences from workbooks/worksheets.	• Instruction utilizes excerpts from familiar text, including the students' own writings.
• Sentence(s) are isolated, and therefore, detached from a bigger meaning or context.	• Sentences come from a bigger piece that provides context for the message.
• The focus is on fixing what is wrong within anonymous sentences.	• The focus is on applying convention skills within personal writing.
• Instruction happens in a separate time of the day/period.	• Instruction happens within writing time/ writer's workshop.
• Teacher conference questions include:	• Teacher conference questions include:
What's the rule about ___ ? *Did you forget anything here?*	*What is it you're trying to say?* *What conventions can help convey that?*

Visual Trigger

Writers utilize tools from the conventions tool box/tool belt to help the reader. These icons are available as JPEGs via the online resource.

Teacher Tip

It's not that convention work *never* happens in isolation. Bell work, morning work, or DOL is acceptable for continued practice. However, it's not where the teaching and instruction should occur.

Launching the Writer's Workshop: Grades 3-12, Kristina Smekens and Maureen Scane
© 2017 Smekens Education Solutions, Inc.

Provide convention instruction within three phases

When teaching a new convention (grammar or mechanics) skill, plan to address it in three mini-lesson phases. Although this often translates into three days of instruction, it may move faster or slower, depending on students' understanding.

PHASE 1: Deconstruct the skill in mentor text.
Reveal the skill within mentor text. Explain the purpose or function of the skill as it pertains to those examples. More than telling students *what* (the convention's rule) a writer should do, explain *why* (the convention's purpose) a writer would use it. Explain *when* a writer would apply it and *how* the skill impacts the message.

During writing time, students find examples of this skill within additional mentor text. They have to be able to notice and name the skill in authentic writing. (NOTE: This excludes worksheets, as every sentence on the worksheet typically utilizes the skill. However, every sentence in a picture book does not. It's a more authentic assessment when students can notice and name the skill when it's found in real text.)

PHASE 2: Reconstruct the skill in previous writings.
Model how to imitate the skill within a previous draft. This lesson includes Think Alouds where the teacher lets students in on the mental choices of a writer.

During writing time, students return to previous pieces and attempt to imitate the convention skill. This is the try-it day. Rather than starting from scratch, students take a topic already fleshed out and imitate the convention skill in the context of the message.

PHASE 3: Construct the skill in new pieces.
Model how to take an idea and craft an original sentence that incorporates that convention skill. This is the apply-it day. After this lesson, teachers hold students accountable for consistent and accurate application of the skill.

During writing time, students construct new sentences that utilize this skill accurately and appropriately.

This three-phase approach to convention instruction honors best-practice and the gradual release of responsibility. Not only is convention instruction *not* to be conducted solely in isolation, it *must* be woven into reading and writing workshops. First a skill is analyzed in mentor text and then imitated within writing.

Video Clip

Watch a Phase 1 mini-lesson about "Juggling Nouns and Pronouns" via the online resource.

Teacher Tip

Download a list of *10 Common Purposes Conventions Serve in Writing* via the online resource.

Teacher Tip

Some teachers understand the three phases of a convention mini-lesson series when it's put into a sports analogy.

PHASE 1 LESSON = Drills at practice: Standing under the basket doing 50 layups, left hand, right hand repeatedly.

PHASE 2 LESSON = Scrimmage: After running a couple of plays, the coach stops and corrects the team.

PHASE 3 LESSON = Game day: It all counts now.

Teacher Tip

Students who read right through punctuation marks, never stopping, pausing, or taking a breath, tend to omit punctuation within their own writing. Consequently, this lesson improves their application of writing conventions *and* their reading fluency.

Mentor Text

...for Hearing Punctuation
20 Odd Ducks, L. Truss
Eats, Shoots & Leaves, L. Truss
Girl's Like Spaghetti, L. Truss
If You Were an Apostrophe, S. Lyons
If You Were a Comma, M. Blaisdell
If You Were an Exclamation Point,
  S. Lyons
If You Were a Period, N. M. Healy
If You Were a Question Mark, S. Lyons
If You Were Quotation Marks,
  M. Blaisdell
Yo! Yes? C. Raschka

Bell-Ringer Idea

Create an alphabet or number passage. The first minutes of class, students are whisper-reading the passage individually accounting for the punctuation marks. The bell-ringer activity wraps up with an in-unison read-aloud of the passage.

HEARING PUNCTUATION

A and B. C? DEF
G. H! I... JK. L?
MN? OP;QR. S
TU! V? W, X,Y. Z!

MINI-LESSON #1: Reread to hear punctuation

For students to apply punctuation marks accurately within their own writing, they need to know more than just the rules. They need to know how the different marks affect the reader's voice.

Reveal the *Hearing Punctuation* chart. More than the rule behind each mark, identify its impact on a reader's fluency. (Start with only the three end marks and the comma. Slowly reveal additional punctuation on the chart later in this lesson or in follow-up lessons.)

When self-editing and whisper-reading (Mini-Lesson #5, p. 36), a writer should *listen* to himself. When his voice stops at the end of a complete thought, he should confirm he placed a period there. If he pauses in a sentence, then he should check for a comma. If writers want readers' voices to stop, pause, get loud, or go up, then the writer has to indicate that with the appropriate punctuation.

Model how this looks and sounds. Project an excerpt of text and read it aloud, emphasizing the period stops, comma pauses, volume changes, etc. Each time, reference that the voice change is because of a punctuation mark.

Reveal a previous draft. The teacher will read it aloud the way it was meant to sound. Confirm that each sentence has the marks to match the read-aloud voice. (NOTE: Choose a draft that has some missing or inaccurate punctuation in order to model the editing process, too.)

Depending on the success of the lesson, consider revealing a few more punctuation marks within the chart and their impacts on the reader's voice. Model the *Read Up, Write Down* strategy (Mini-Lesson #5, p. 36) while self-editing a second writing sample.

Independent Writing:

Using previous drafts, students will self-edit for punctuation using the *Read Up, Write Down* strategy. Remind students that when they find punctuation errors, they should turn back into writers, lay the piece down on the desk, and make the changes. Then they should turn back into readers and lift, whisper, and track.

Read UP. **Write** DOWN.

1. **LIFT** THE PAPER TO READ IT.
   Lay it down to make a change.
2. **WHISPER** READ ALOUD.
   Move your lips!
3. **TRACK** THE WORDS.
   Touch them when you read them.

MINI-LESSON **#2: Introduce a** *Speaking Punctuation* **procedure**

Writers choose punctuation when drafting a piece in order to communciate the intended message. *I love spring!* is different from *I LOVE spring!* and *I love spring?* Each of those sentences produces a different message.

Consequently, punctuation needs to become a focus during the composing step of the writing process— not just the editing stage.

To highlight punctuation within a first draft, introduce a new class procedure— *Speaking Punctuation.*

Explain that for short stints of time, students will engage in conversations with peers, and when they do, they will have to insert the appropriate punctuation as if they were writing down the conversation. For example, if explaining a weekend activity, the teacher might say, *I went to my uncle's (apostrophe s) house and helped plant trees, (comma) bushes, (comma) and flowers (period).*

It seems a little awkward at first, but it doesn't take long for students to get the hang of it.

Model a second example. *After we play (capital S) Speaking (capital P) Punctuation, (comma) we will read silently within our library books (period).*

The benefit to this activity is that the students are thinking about their punctuation marks when talking, which translates into them thinking about their punctuation marks during first-draft writing, too.

Identify a topic for the students to engage in a whole-class conversation. Every time someone speaks, he identifies the sentence punctuation while moving through the sentence.

Independent Writing:

Pairs practice *Speaking Punctuation* while the teacher eavesdrops on conversations.

Teacher Tip

Dictation apps and websites encourage students to speak sentences with the necessary punctuation marks in the first draft.

ONLINE RESOURCES

Evernote App—Free app that turns audio files into texts that sync with Evernote.

Voice Assistant App— For 99¢, this app can send transcriptions straight to a wireless printer.

Dragon Dictation 2.0 — Dictate a lengthy paragraph; the text appears after you finish. This new version auto-saves in Chrome and exports to Dropbox and Google Drive.

dictation.io— Free online speech recognition software powered by Google Chrome.

MINI-LESSON #3: Indent for new information

Students need to know when to indent or start a new paragraph. It's *not* about counting the number of sentences.

An indent serves an important purpose for the reader. It's a visual indication that there is a shift in information. It does not matter how many sentences are written. When the topic shifts to a new facet, then an indent acknowledges that. (See Follow-Up Lesson for breaking paragraphs with a new line versus an indent.)

Reveal the *3 Common Reasons to Indent a Paragraph* handout. Thoroughly discuss the different instances when information shifted.

1. Subtopic Shift. When the facts, information, details, or ideas shift to another facet of the topic, it's time for a new paragraph. Indent when a new character or person is introduced. Indent for each new event or happening.

Reveal example paragraphs from recently read mentor text. Describe the subtopic of one paragraph and the subtopic of the next one. Define *that* as a shift in information and rationale for a paragraph break.

2. Setting Shift. When there is a shift in time, location, day, or date, writers alert their readers with an indent. Think of it like a video camera. When a different scene or setting is in the viewfinder, then there should have been a paragraph break. A more abstract facet of setting is mood. But when the mood or emotional energy changes, it usually requires a paragraph break, too.

Reveal example paragraphs from recently read mentor text. Describe the setting of one paragraph and the setting of the next one. Define *that* as a shift in information.

3. Speaker Shift. Every time a character (dialogue) or individual (quote) speaks, a new paragraph is needed. When every line of a back-and-forth conversation isn't labeled with a speaker, the reader still knows who is talking because of this paragraph rule. There should also be a new paragraph when the writing goes from a character/expert quote back to the body paragraphs/narrator.

Reveal example paragraphs from recently read mentor text. Describe the speaker of one paragraph and the speaker of the next one. Define *that* as a shift in information.

Independent Writing:

Return to previous drafts and proofread for missing indents. Add the ¶ symbol and label *subtopic, setting,* or *speaker* to indicate the reason for the paragraph break.

Launching the Writer's Workshop: Grades 3-12, Kristina Smekens and Maureen Scane
© 2017 Smekens Education Solutions, Inc.

MINI-LESSON #4: Apply quotation marks around speech

Much of a story is presented by a narrator— the person describing the event. However, occasionally characters "talk." Within informative, persuasive, and argumentative writing, the author (the student) presents his ideas/thinking with the occasional expert quote included.

This juggling of "speakers" can confuse the reader if convention rules aren't followed. Writers must indicate to their readers when someone besides the author or narrator is "talking."

Review the evolution of a quotation mark. In Greek times, playwrights did not use quote marks to tell the actor what to say. Quote marks hadn't been "invented" yet. Rather, the writers drew a pair of lips around the words an actor was to say. These lips represented an actor opening his mouth and speaking. Playwrights drew a second pair of lips to indicate when the speaking part was over and the actor should close his mouth.

Eventually a shorthand version was created— the quotation marks. Present-day quotation marks represent the pair of lips. The left one indicates the mouth/lips open and the right set concludes the speaking with the closing of the mouth/lips.

Only the words that come out of a character or expert's mouth are within the "lip" marks. The adjacent words and phrases that indicate *who* said it and/or *how* it was said are *not* to be included in the quotation marks. These descriptions are provided by the author/narrator. They are known as speaker tags and attribution. Since these phrases were *not* actually spoken out of the character or expert's lips, then they are not to be included within the quotation marks.

The accurate application of quotation marks is an unspoken agreement between readers and writers. When students don't follow this writing rule, the reader struggles to differentiate between what was said by the narrator/author versus characters/experts.

Independent Writing:

Students sit in teams of three. Provide passages from mentor text that include a combination of quotations and narration. Students decide who's character A, who's character B, and who's the narrator. They read the excerpt aloud, depending on the speaker. Each time character A or B speaks, that student will also make air quotes to signal the opening and closing of his mouth.

Follow-Up Lesson

Each new quote/speaker indicates a shift in information. Therefore, there should be a paragraph break with each new quote (Mini-Lesson #3, p. 124).

Follow-Up Lesson

Within informative, persuasive, and argumentative units, combine this mini-lesson with Mini-Lessons #12-#13, pp. 71-72. Teach students how to discern when an expert's words are powerful enough to quote or when they should just be paraphrased.

Follow-Up Lesson

Within persuasive, argumentative, and informative writing, teach students how to incorporate source citations before the quote, at the end of the quote, and in the middle of long quotes (Mini-Lesson #14, p. 73).

Follow-Up Lesson

Within a narrative writing unit, teach students how to punctuate character dialogue that sounds natural. This means there are typically sentence fragments between the quotation marks (Mini-Lesson #2, p. 113).